A GUIDE TO HEALTH CARE JOINT VENTURES

I. Donald Snook, Jr.
President
Presbyterian—University of Pennsylvania
Medical Center
Philadelphia, Pennsylvania

Edita M. Kaye
President
Kaye Associates, Inc.
New York, New York

AN ASPEN PUBLICATION®
Aspen Publishers, Inc.

1987

Rockville, Maryland
Royal Tunbridge Wells

Library of Congress Cataloging in Publication Data

Snook, I. Donald.
A guide to health care joint ventures.

"An Aspen publication."
Includes bibliographies and index.
1. Hospitals — Business management. 2. Joint ventures. I. Kaye, Edita. II. Title.
[DNLM: 1. Health Facilities — organization & administration.
2. Hospital Administration. 3. Multi-Institutional Systems.
WX 157.4 S673g]
RA971.3.S576 1986 362.1'1'068 86–22195
ISBN: 0–87189–609–5

Editorial Services: Ruth Bloom

Library of Congress Catalog Card Number: 86–22195
ISBN: 0–87189–609–5

Printed in the United States of America

1 2 3 4 5

This book is dedicated to all the players in the health care game—from the biggest to the smallest, from the most innovative to the most conservative. It also is dedicated to their users—the public staying healthier through these changing times.

Table of Contents

Introduction: How To Use This Book

This book is a primer, a compilation of information on joint ventures in health care, all between two covers. It is very much like a hero sandwich—stuffed with lots of goodies—not everything to everybody's taste. It is designed for you, the health care administrator, to read through and to work through with your own people in order to get a sense of which of the myriad of joint ventures is right for your hospital.

However, this primer is just a road map, a guide. It is not a destination. It highlights the main intersections, red flags the potholes, and points out the detours.

The field of joint ventures is fluid and dynamic, and the successful readers and users of this book will take what is offered here and run with it . . . to the benefit of their own facilities and the public and physicians they serve.

Part I

Joint Ventures: What They Are, How They Operate

Chapter 1

Opportunities for Joint Ventures

We must drop the idea that change comes slowly. It does ordinarily—in part because we think it does. Today, changes must come fast; and we must adjust our mental habits, so that we can accept comfortably the idea of stopping one thing and beginning another overnight. We must discard the idea that past routine, past ways of doing things, are probably the best ways. On the contrary, we must assume that there is probably a better way to do almost everything. We must stop assuming that a thing which has never been done before probably cannot be done at all.

Donald M. Nelson

CHANGE IS TO SHIFT ONE'S POSITION AND BE BRUISED IN A NEW PLACE.

Washington Irving

HIGHLIGHTS

- All About Change: The Good, the Bad, the Unavoidable
- The Business of Health: What Is It?
- Enter the High-Tech/Megadollar Age
- Competition: The Race Belongs to the Swift and Creative
- Management: The Weakest Link, or the Strongest?
- Strategic Planning: The Toss of the Dice
- Marketing: Basic Lessons in Sales
- The Future: A Peek into the Health Care Crystal Ball

1

The word is change. Dynamics. Flux. Chaos. Uncertainty is king. And for health care professionals the world has become a shifting, turbulent mass of unknowns. The gameboard has been redrawn. The players are different. The polite Marquis of Queensbury rules for gentlemen have been usurped by the rough-and-tumble "anything goes" of American business.

Welcome to the real world.

> There are two ways to deal with this scenario: 1. to take the ostrich approach and hope that when the dust clears, everything will remain as it once was. 2. to take the "where there is change there is also opportunity" approach, recognizing that nothing remains constant and that pluses are sprinkled liberally throughout the landscape, like colored eggs on the White House lawn at Easter, for those with the vision and courage to find them.

That's about where the health care industry and its professionals now stand—some rolling their eyes heavenward hoping for divine intervention, others peering under bushes, running up hills, working up a sweat to find the golden eggs of opportunity. And it is the opportunists, the visionaries, the risk-takers who are creating a new health care industry that will be nothing like the old and that will benefit every component of society with which it interfaces—from patients, to physicians, to administrators, to other businesses. The operating policy of this new health care industry will simply be: "Go for it." Those who do will be pleasantly surprised, those who don't will find themselves in an industrial graveyard, alongside the manufacturers of the once-famous buggy whip.

WHAT IS THE BUSINESS OF HEALTH?

Are we making those buggy whips, when everyone is driving automobiles?

Ask anyone on the street to name the top three businesses in America today and they will talk about cars, computers, cosmetics, fashion—everything but health care. Why? Because for centuries health and medicine were not considered businesses at all, but services. Doctors provided care, medicine, bandages, inoculations. Medical researchers provided cures for horrible, devastating diseases, and hospitals provided beds, nurses, operating rooms, treatment facilities, and emergency care. Not one of those elements was ever considered a business, particularly not by those directly involved. Even those who have made a life career in health still carry around the Marcus Welby image or the Florence Nightingale view. Very romantic, but very unrealistic in today's world.

One of the toughest changes that faces health care is to make that mindset change from service and mission to profits and new markets. And the two, service and mission, profits and new markets do not necessarily have to be at variance with one another. There is room for both.

HOSPITAL, KNOW THYSELF

> Yogi Berra, that famous American philosopher once said, "If you don't know where you are going, you could end up somewhere else."

If you as a hospital manager were asked, "What business are you in?," what would your answer be?

a. The business of providing top-quality, cutting-edge, high-technology institutional medical care.
b. The business of cutting-edge, cost-effective, high-quality medical services.
c. The business of health care, period.
d. All of the above.

If your answer was *d* (all of the above), you have at least a grasp on the magnitude of what is fast becoming an entirely new industry—health care. To carry the Yogi Berra image one step further, to know where you are going is critical, but just as critical is knowing where you are. The operating question, once those two vectors have been identified, is: Can you get there from here?

Let's see where "here" really is for the hospital industry as this moment in time.

THE SPARE PARTS BUSINESS

What exactly does the hospital industry do today? Unquestionably it is, and since 1954 has been involved in "spare parts" medicine. In 1954 the first kidney transplant revolutionized the health care field and opened up a cookie jar of new, exciting, cutting-edge services. That first transplant gave stratospheric boundaries to what essentially had been a place to be patched up and medicated.

The possibilities were endless, and the health care industry to its credit and innovation rapidly moved ahead. To where? To the Dr. Barney Clark heart transplant and to research on Baby Doe. In fact, the hospital industry is better at "putting parts in and taking parts out" than any other industry.

THE HIGH-TECH GAME OF CHANCE

The corollary to this "spare parts" process was the simultaneous development of high-tech diagnostic and other tools. Every day we have newer and better instumentation and computerization. Even the jargon has shifted and health care workers find themselves talking about such sci-fi phenomena as lasers, ultrasound, magnetic resonance imaging (MRI)—words unheard of a few short years ago.

> So while the automobile industry, for example, is still talking about trunk space, head room, and cylinders, the health care industry has moved light years beyond the scalpel, the x-ray, and the "booster shot." In short, new products are being developed and health care professionals are being carried along on the wave of high-tech development in which the industry undoubtedly is a leader.

Lasers—the acronym for light amplification by stimulated emission of radiation—have revolutionized outpatient surgery. There was a time, just yesterday it seems, when surgeons were the undisputed "cutters." All invasive procedures were performed by the men and women in scrub suits with scalpels in their hands. No more. Scalpels are being replaced with laser rods and surgery is fast, painless, and bloodless. Better yet, recovery time is faster and there is significantly reduced risk of infection and tissue trauma.

But, even as you read this, the laser is involved in a great debate: Should nonsurgeons be allowed to use this high-tech scalpel on patients and, if so, what happens to the surgical department as we have known it?

> The MRI already has moved the nuclear age into most major communities and is rapidly supplementing, if not replacing, computerized axial tomography (CAT) scan. The develoment of this high-tech modality has pushed the industry's ability to diagnose light years ahead of its ability to treat.

Most patients are beginning to understand the implications of such a development for their own lives. However frustrating as this may be for the patients, it is doubly so for physicians, and pressure is increasing on the research component of the health care industry to play catch-up with itself.

While these are not the only two high-tech developments on the health care scene, they serve as excellent examples of the changes that a single product, such as the laser or the MRI, has caused in an entire industry. If health care were faced only with assimilating treatment and diagnostic changes, it would do so with less anguish than it is facing today. The reason is that the problems are multiple. They only begin with high technology—then simultaneously encompass traditional business/corporate areas such as marketing, product, and service development, plus that biggest challenge of them all: competition.

DO IT TO THEM BEFORE THEY DO IT TO YOU

The trade press in the mid-1980s has been been filled with the specter of competition. Everyone is in the race—doctors with doctors, doctors with hospitals, hospitals with their own medical staffs, hospitals with hospitals, even hospitals with department stores that are pushing health three aisles down from sundry household items and one aisle over from the travel agency and in-store cash machine. It's as though a giant treadmill has been engaged and everyone in health care is speed-walking and not really getting far. It's time to stop.

Hospitals, in particular, have found themselves far removed from the traditional friendly competition with others to attract the superstar physicians. One reason, of course is the deliberate strategy of federal policymakers who feel that by artificially stimulating competition through legislative means, a curb can be built around the rising costs of health care. Hospitals have used resource acquisition as the basis of their market behavior, and nonprice rivalry has been their dominant form of competition. No more.

> Competition is a major component of hospitals' strategic planning and certainly a big chunk of the real business of health care today. Competition is not going to go away in the near future. It is coloring, sometimes in frustrating shades of opaque graylike fog in a British murder mystery, the clear, firm lines of the health care industry of tomorrow. Which brings the health care industry squarely up against its own management capabilities.

MANAGEMENT: WEAKEST LINK OR STRONGEST?

There are two kinds of managers: the ones who manage change and the ones that let change manage them. As far as the health care manager of today is concerned, the jury is still out on which group is the dominant. What is evident is the fact that so many competent, skilled, and able hospital administrators have difficulty planning for the future. Why?

Just take a look at what each day brings to an administrator: a decision on doctors' parking spaces, malfunctioning sterilizing equipment, and endless meetings with subordinates, medical staff, and trustees. That's the typical mix of the typical administrator's in-basket. The management of problems is the operating style.

Now take a look at the mix on the calendar of a successful corporate chief executive officer (CEO). There are high-level strategy meetings, marketing and advertising decisions, in-depth market and demographic analyses, constant acquisitions and divestitures, and a keen interest and time for research and development.

> These changing times call for less paper shuffling and more, much more, time, energy, and creativity devoted to setting objectives, studying the marketplace, and establishing goals.

While we health care administrators might scream "unfair," the fact remains that the job description has changed. Leaders, not high-level clerks, are called for.

> Vision is seeing things invisible.
>
> *Jonathan Swift*

Today's winners in the industry of health will have to develop those characteristics so carefully cultivated by other industries in a volatile market:

- Planning for the future will be the biggest time drain. Setting objectives, researching changes, understanding the impact of legislative reform, staying in touch with other, alternative providers and their contributions, and always taking advantage of every change, every shift, every opportunity for their own facility.
- Motivating staff resistant to change will be a major part of the job, clearly and confidently identifying the hospital's objectives, and getting the best out of personnel in difficult times.
- Identifying and promoting the aces in the hospital inventory of services and discarding the tens, jacks, and even queens that clutter up the hand—putting all the hospital's eggs sometimes in just one or two well-constructed baskets and becoming the very best, not necessarily the biggest in a certain field.
- Asking those tough questions and being prepared to deal creatively with the answers. What do our physicians really want? What do our patients really want? Are we delivering? Do we even know whether we are doing the right job for them?
- Inventing and implementing new products in spite of all opposition. Just because grandfather did it this way, and so did good old dad,

doesn't mean the same formula will work today. Understanding that America is aging, that it is fixated on youth and good health and food and exercise, and that the key issue is developing products and services that make the hospital the main supplier of the real and imagined needs of the nation.

Ask yourself: Why should people go to exercise gyms and diet clubs—why not to a hospital? After all, aren't both servicing bodies and promoting health? Why should the restaurants be in shopping malls when good nutrition is key to health. Why not in hospitals?

> Think of the possibilities: the hospital as entertainment facility, spa, recreation facility, community center. Why not?

Certainly one of the biggest of health care businesses is the business of managing its own future. Fast on the heels of that component is the new business of marketing—a legitimate business in its own right and one that must be integrated with health.

MARKETING: THE FINE ART OF SELLING GOODS THAT WON'T COME BACK TO CUSTOMERS WHO WILL

For corporate America, marketing is respectable. For much of the health care industry, on the contrary, marketing is (or has been) a dirty word. It still smacks of the snake-oil salesman, the drummer, the peddler, the Fuller Brush man, and the pitiful image of Willy Loman in "Death of a Salesman." But, like it or not, marketing is here to stay in health care, as in every other business that hopes to grow to survive in the contemporary marketplace.

> Your market has a free choice, and only by supplying what the market wants and not by your efforts to impose your merchandise, will you get your maximum share of the market's potential.
>
> *Walter H. Lowry*

Marketing is one of the most misunderstood blocks in the organization chart:

- Marketing is not selling.
- It is not advertising.
- It is not public relations.
- It is not merchandising. It is all of those.

Marketing itself is a broad umbrella term covering certain activities that singly and in combination with one another stimulate clients to purchase a product or service. The component parts of marketing are:

- Sales: This includes selling via direct mail, telemarketing, door-to-door and any other activity that generates an order.
- Advertising: This includes such elements as ads in magazines and newspapers and on billboards and posters, stuffers in invoices, and radio and television commercials.
- Public Relations. This involves mostly nonpaid promotion, including community seminars and workships, fund-raising, articles in magazines and newspapers, interviews on radio or television, patient education programs, staff training programs, client relations, trustee luncheons, orientations, and the like.
- Merchandising: This includes all the different packagings for the hospital's products and services—the women's center, the diagnostic facilities, the special programs for alcohol and substance abuse, the innovative uses of space and the delineation of service areas.

Marketing no longer is an overly powdered, aging lady of the evening skilled in the arts of concealment, nor is the centuries-old "let the buyer beware" the marketing slogan. Marketing has become respectable.

> Marketing is both the art and science of determining what is needed and then filling that need.

Health care, with its long history of professionalism and attention to quality, is at the forefront of making marketing an even more integral and necessary function of business—even the business of health.

HOSPITALS OF TOMMORROW: TRENDS, PREDICTIONS

> The future is "the shape of things to come."
>
> *H.G. Wells*

But the future is more than a crystal ball. We are given clues to the possible shape of the future in today's present and even in yesterday's past. Examine the trends that even now are shaping the future of the health care industry. Each trend holds within it the seeds of opportunity.

New Patient Configurations

Is there any doubt that this country is becoming older? By the time the apple drops on Times Square in the year 2016, there will be 35 million Americans over the age of 65. The statistics are mind boggling. What will this new wave of geriatric consumers be shopping for?

The New England Journal of Medicine reports that by the time a person reaches the age of 85 (and many of us will achieve that bonus beyond the biblical three-score years and ten), assistance in just managing the basics of day-to-day living will be in demand.

Help to get dressed. Hot food. Errands. Simple, mundane activities will become impossible without help. Almost four out of ten persons over 85 need this type of help just to exist and the 85-plus group is the fastest growing age group and will be into the 21st century. Just think of the opportunities.

Corporate Reorganization

If hospitals are to grab off new opportunities, they must be organized for action. Let's suppose that an opportunity presented itself to a hospital to start an ambulance service in a joint venture with an existing for-profit service or other hospital.

- How does the hospital handle the new business from an organizational standpoint?
- Should a new corporate entity be formed?
- Should it be for profit or not profit?

- How will the new business mesh with the existing mission?
- Who will manage the new venture?
- Where will the funds come from?
- Where will profits or revenues go?
- How will the venture be marketed?
- Who will do the necessary hiring and firing?

Tomorrow's hospital must be a lean, mean business machine. Able to move into opportunities fast, the organizational structure must be flexible to allow for speed. That is the winning formula and the trend in business that is evident in every industry. How about your hospital? How fast can you move it, organizationally speaking?

Social/Demographic Trends

The rapidly changing trends in society and in its demographics pose questions and challenges for hospital administrators:

- How much do you know about shifting population patterns?
- Are people moving into or out of cities?
- Are more children being born today than 20 years ago, or fewer?
- Is the population well educated or is a high school diploma the norm?
- Is society mainly white, Anglo-Saxon, and Protestant (WASP) or is it mainly minorities?
- Is English the dominant language or are other languages being used with greater frequency? For example, in Philadelphia since 1974 160,000 Hispanics moved into the city, and as recently as 1984, 55,000 Southeast Asians have swelled the city's population.
- How many women of childbearing age work fulltime?
- How many households have two wage earners?
- What about television habits—what are people watching?
- What new magazines and books are hot?
- What is going on in religion? In many inner-city areas there used to be churches, Ys, and other social agencies but they have become fewer and fewer. In fact, in many inner-city neighborhoods, only the police and fire stations and hospitals remain as social institutions.

- How is economics affecting health care industry? Producing more missiles and warheads on the West Coast has an effect on Medicaid in the large Eastern states.
- What about political trends? Is the political climate friendly or hostile to the health care business?

If you can't identify these social and demographic trends you will not be able to respond to shifting needs in your own immediate market sphere. It follows that you won't be able to service your own base effectively and may lose it to hospitals that can.

The Outpatient

There will always be coronary care units (CCUs), intensive care units (ICUs), stepdown beds, and operating rooms for inpatient surgery, but the trend to fewer and fewer medical/surgical beds is evident. It looks as though the clients of the future will be outpatients. One survey found that "the number of hospitals reporting increased outpatient use rose to 83 percent in 1985, up from 70 percent in 1984. Although the trend is nationwide, it's most pronounced in the Southeast, followed by the West." The same report found that the largest increases in outpatient use came in hospitals with 100 to 199 beds, with 20 percent more reporting increases over the previous year.

Data collected on an ongoing basis by the American Hospital Association echo the trend. "Between 1980 and 1985 ambulatory surgery procedures increased more than 100 percent, representing 28 percent of total surgical procedures in hospitals. Many observers estimate that as much as sixty percent of all surgeries will be performed on an outpatient basis within the next few years" (*Hospitals,* July 20, 1986, p. 46). Outpatient surgery rose 77 percent between 1979 and 1983 at hospitals nationwide while inpatient procedures fell 7 percent during the same period. While there have been some concerns that postoperative complications might make outpatient surgery riskier, both the American Medical Association in 1971 and the American College of Surgeons in 1981 endorsed the practice.

> The outpatient is here to stay and, judging by the sheer numbers, to grow.

Satellites

The overall trend in American business is to satellites. Look at banks, food stores, department stores, and almost every other service you can think of. There are more satellites here on earth than are spinning around in space. In this case, health care follows the corporate lead. Satellites proliferate. An industry report predicts that 3,000 urgicenters (a form of hospital satellite) will log in 45 million patient visits a year and deliver $1.9 billion worth of health care by the late 1980s.

Programs Are In, Buildings Are Out

Expanding the "health zone" is another critical trend to be watched carefully. Look at heart surgery. When will the industry stop building operating rooms to do open-heart surgery? The fact is that one out of two patients who suffers a heart attack is going to die as a result. Yet how many hospitals send a representative into an office building and say to a high-risk executive, "What can we do as a hospital to keep you from having a heart attack?" When we do this, and mean it, we are taking advantage of a trend. Hospitals would be entering the "health zone" of program planning, not construction.

Look at the free-standing cancer clinics. Plunked down in the middle of hospital parking lots, they are an impressive group. Filled with equipment, machinery, computers, arrays of drugs, and starched staff, what are they really providing? A building. No! A program. In the cancer clinics, where are the hospice coordinators, the psychologists, the family therapists, and the clergy? They are providing the human services, those critical elements of a health program, not just a facility.

Joint Ventures

> "Everybody's doin' it, doin' it, doin' it . . , " the old song says, and that doesn't mean the Lindy—it means joint ventures.

Look around. Joint ventures are the synergistic relationships between companies in which one plus one can and often does equal three. The joint venture, as this book describes, is the straw that will allow hospitals to breathe in the increasingly thick, competitive air of business.

Hospitals with hospitals, hospitals with their own medical staffs, with groups of physicians, with drug companies, with for-profit corporations, with venture capitalists—the couplings are endless, exciting, and, if structured correctly, profitable both in a quantitative financial sense to satisfy the number crunchers, and in a qualitative sense to satisfy the professionals concerned with the quality of health care.

How many of these broad trends fill the files of today's hospital chief executive officer (CEO)? How carefully does hospital management monitor general social as well as industry tends? The skill in forecasting, predicting, and educated guessing will separate the winners from the losers in the race to cope with change.

Now we come to some of the specific opportunities that are growing out of the trends of today that will continue to emerge from the trends of tomorrow.

OPPORTUNITIES FOR NEW VENTURES

> Contrary to the commonly accepted belief, it is the risk element in our capitalistic system which produces an economy of security. Risk brings out ingenuity and resourcefulness which insure the success of enough ventures to keep the economy growing and secure.
>
> *Robert Rawls*

It is a given that hospitals are well into a risk phase that has been the hallmark of American business since the earliest beginnings. With increased risks come increased rewards—and increased possibilities for failure. However, a careful reading of trends, market analysis, and good old-fashioned gut feelings will take hospital administrators far in launching new businesses that have a better-than-average chance for survival and growth.

Here are some possibles that work.

Medical Hotel

The "hotel hospital" is an illustration of a new product at work. When diagnosis related groups (DRGs) came along, hospitals had a challenge. All of a sudden, by the stroke of a pen, Medicare no longer was paying a hospital cost of $750/day for keeping patients horizontal. The government informed hospitals that they now were going to receive a fixed amount of reimbursement per case.

The reaction? Presbyterian University of Pennsylvania Medical Center, for example, looked at the resultant problem and wondered:

> "Do all the patients in the hospital have to be actually in the hospital to receive hospital services?"

A good question. Presbyterian next reviewed its medical records and interviewed physicians, patients' families, and patients. The result? It discovered that 20 percent of the surgical patients could be somewhere else as long as they could receive hospital services.

What to do with all these data? How to turn them to the hospital's advantage? The answer: Open a medical hotel, or HotelHospital. A hotel hospital will not solve all of an institution's problems nor is it a quick fix for industrywide difficulties. But it is a legitimate species of delivery that works.

In the case of Presbyterian Medical Center, its HotelHospital was a separate facility just 20 yards from the main building. (Such facility also could be part of an existing hospital, such as a wing or an empty floor.) It is a private—very private—hotel with 24-hour on-the-floor "medical concierge coverage." The concierge monitors the daily medical activities of guests/patients and tracks them at all times. In addition there is a gourmet restaurant and all the facilities of any luxury hotel in any major city. All this, and for $500 a day less than the cost of being an inpatient in the Medical Center itself. Truly an exciting new health care product, of and for patients of the 1980s and beyond.

Nursing Homes

Tremendous opportunities for new product development exist in nursing homes. An April 1985 study reports that for affluent elderly persons considering entering retirement housing, the availability and quality of health care services are major criteria in their decision-making process. Another study finds that 50 percent of the senior citizens surveyed selected a supportive care facility based primarily on the quality of health care offered, not on the quality of physical accommodations. This makes hospitals the prime providers of health care in the business of supplying services and facilities for the elderly.

> Just look at the numbers. Approximately 35,000 nursing home beds are under construction every year. At the same time, 25,000 a year disappear through obsolescence or bad management that often leads to bankruptcy. That's the amount of product out there.

Let's look at the demand. It is estimated that 400,000 nursing home beds for those 75 years of age and older will be needed annually by 1990. Even if the number of beds were to increase by 20,000 annually, occupancy still would reach 100 percent before the end of the decade. That's the need.

Now, let's look at the market surveys. What exactly do the elderly require or want in a nursing home? Surprisingly enough, what they themselves want is very different from what their families think they want. The elderly want what the rest of us want—quality of life, and to them that means companionship. Their families, on the other hand, often feel that the greatest need of an elderly relative is security. The challenge in the health care industry is to meet both needs.

This is a perfect fit for hospitals. They already have available the medical care that is critical. They have the staff. More and more of them have the space as beds empty out. Most important of all, hospitals already have the image in the public's mind of being places that care. With just a little planning, market research, and creative use of space, hospitals could develop innovative programs and facilities for an aging population, building products not only to prolong their own fiscal lives but to grow and prosper as an industry.

Quality-of-Life Campuses

In the elderly market, there are programs that could become products for joint ventures, particularly supplying the affluent elderly. Imagine a complex, complete with residential, hospital, Hotel Hospital, day care center, comprehensive outpatient rehabilitation facilities (CORFs)—a village for the affluent elderly. What an exciting venture for hospitals to become involved in supplying a market need and developing a new health care product at the same time.

Home Health Services

Another service area ripe for development by hospitals is the home health care sector. According to National Research Corporation report, 50 percent of all the hospitals in the country already provide some form of home health care services to patients and another 25 percent have plans on their drawing boards.

Examine the trends and the opportunities linked to them in this product area. Americans are living longer, women who traditionally remained in the home to care first for children and then the sick and elderly, now are in the work force or have moved across the country and are not available for home care.

Now, examine the needs. Many patients need short-term postoperative care. Hospitals have financial incentives to discharge patients sooner. After a procedure, outpatient surgery puts people in their own homes the same day.

Examine the opportunities. There is need for expanded home health care, not only by professional nursing staffs but by home managers who have basic skills and who run the errands, prepare the meals, and tidy up for patients who are not sick enough for full time in-hospital care but not well enough to look after themselves.

This need encompasses more than professional visiting nurses. It includes the development of home medical equipment, home monitoring equipment, home testing devices. In fact, one research firm estimates that annual revenues from home health care products and services will grow from the $3.9 billion of 1983 to $13.8 billion by 1990. "One forecaster called it the "third largest industry in America today. . . . The number of patients referred to home care has increased 37 percent since Medicare prospective pricing was enacted in 1983." (*Hospitals,* April 30, 1986). At the AHA home care conference in February 1985, data revealed that 90 percent of the participants planned some sort of joint venture/partnership (*Hospitals,* May 20, 1986).

Where will the revenues from home health care be generated?

- Visiting nurse services. These traditional efforts still are cash producers.
- In-home monitoring devices. A monitoring device developed by RCA in its Princeton, N.J., labs works like a hand-held radar to measure heart beat and respiration rates. The user points it at the subject and the box sends out two weak microwave beams that bounce back and produce digital readings within five seconds. This is just one version of lifeline and other personal monitoring devices being developed.

- Infusion therapies. These include intravenous feeding, intravenous antibiotic therapy, and continuous intravenous chemotherapy. Chemotherapy can and will be delivered in the home. Hospitals are filled with cancer patients. Nutrition (both enteral and parenteral feeding) shows promise of increasing and can be managed under a home program. One estimate for the infusion market indicates that 10,400 intravenous feeding patients were under treatment at home in 1983 and the prognosis for the future is positive. Research shows that the patient universe using this type of home care will grow 191 percent by 1990. It has been noted in *Modern Healthcare* (February 14, 1986) that the infusion therapies market had revenues of $277 million in 1984 and that will grow by 33 percent annually through 1988 when revenues are expected to reach $1 billion.
- Durable medical equipment. There now are durable medical equipment companies that are specializing in in-the-home respirators. "Emphysema is the fastest growing cause of death in the United States," says a spokesman for Baxter Travenol. An annual growth rate of 12 percent to 15 percent in respiratory therapy equipment is predicted by 1990. What was an $878 million industry in the early 1980s is predicted by industry analysis to hit $1.9 billion by 1990. Why shouldn't hospitals cut a slice of that need and product for themselves and their patient universe?
- In-home self-diagnostic testing. This is a major trend in medical services. Experts predict that, for example, in vitro diagnostic testing of patients at home will increase 27 percent each year at least until 1986 and 1990. Home health services should be involved with this movement and so should forward-thinking hospitals.
- Home biofeedback. Biofeedback techniques and programs will be leaving hospitals and moving into the home to help with pain management as yet another opportunity for hospitals expanding their product base.

Mental Illness

Excluding hospital administrators (although there are some days . . .) 24 million Americans suffer from some sort of mental illness. The technology for treating mental illness is conservatively estimated, by health care statisticians to be 150 years behind high-tech surgery. Visiting a closed psychiatric unit is not pleasant. More than 200 years ago, a French physician, Dr. Panel, took the chains off the lunatics in Paris. Today, our mentally ill patients are back in a different form of chains: drug therapy. How many schizophrenic patients have been treated and sent back into society as functioning? The answer: Very few indeed. There are great opportunities in the development of programs for the mentally ill.

Programs also are needed to treat the million of Americans who at one time or another in their lives experience emotional trauma. Where can they go for interim help? Isn't a hospital a natural, logical facility?

It is estimated by health care statisticians that 5 to 20 percent of college-age women have anorexia nervosa (an eating disorder). Look around, is there a college or university near your facility? Is there a market for a new product in this area that can and should be developed?

The Corporate Product

In 1983 Americans spent $355 billion for health care, representing a record 10.8 percent of the gross national product (GNP). In that same year, medical expenditures per person averaged slightly under $1,500, also a record.

> Health care now eats $1 out of every $9 that an American worker earns and the typical employee works little more than 30 days—one month—just to pay for health insurance illness expenses each year. The numbers are staggering.

The Commerce Department reports that private employers' contributions to group health insurance rose from $69.5 billion to $82 billion in the single year from 1982 to 1983—an 18 percent increase. Look at the opportunities for new products and services sold directly to the corporate market, particularly in prevention and employee education. Add to that the fact that only 50 percent of medical and health bills in the United States are paid for by Medicare and Medicaid (government) and you are left with the staggering information that the other 50 percent of all health and medical costs are paid for by employers.

Look at these data from the company point of view. The objective of all companies is to increase profits and reduce costs. Health care costs are an increasing, not decreasing, figure on the books, a drain on profits, and are boosting operating expenses significantly.

Don't you think corporations would welcome ways to reduce those medical costs? Wouldn't you if you were sitting in an executive's chair in the company across the street? In fact, if the CEOs of the top 100 corporations in this country were assembled and a hospital administrator asked them, "what can I do for you?" the answer would be a unanimous, "Cut my health care costs. Don't give me more services, just cut my costs."

> A recent survey of Fortune 500 companies reports that of all the cost-containment strategies employed by industry, ambulatory surgery ranks first, followed by home care, health maintenance organizations (HMOs), self-insurance programs, second opinions for surgery, utilization review programs, representation on hospital boards, greater cost sharing, business coalitions, inhouse corporate medical programs, and preadmission reviews.

Using this information as a clear statement of companies' needs, hospitals should be able to develop strategies and programs that fit those demands. If the hospital industry wants to serve business, it must meet the expressed needs somehow. The question is: How do you meet those business and industry needs beyond offering discounts on medical services?

The answer lies in examining specific needs and filling them.

> - Increased ambulatory surgery. Business wants more of this service because ambulatory surgery is less costly than overnight hospital stays.
> - Outpatient testing. Outpatient care is here to stay. Of patients being tested in MRI centers, 95 percent will be outpatients. Increase your outpatient offerings to industry and you will increase you patient base.
> - Wellness programs. This is a biggie—a huge area of potential product for innovative hospitals. For one example, just look at a stop-smoking program for a local industry.

Industry surveys indicate that smokers cost the United States $35 billion-year. The cost of loss of productivity while workers are being treated for smoking-related problems such as cardiac arrest, emphysema, coronary artery disease and cancer are estimated at $27 to up to $61 billion a year.

> One company made a dramatic and profitable move to try to eliminate those costs. The New York Telephone Company has 88,000 employees. In the mid-1970s it made a corporate commitment to a wellness program, including a major smoke cessation program. Ten years later it had some very hard data on its employees. After spending as much as $5.5 million a year on these programs, the company reported its total savings in health care came to $8.2 million, with $700,000 of it from the smoke cessation program alone.

Companies are well aware that they are spending more than $700 million-year to replace the more than 200,000 men between the ages of 45 and 65 who are killed or disabled by coronary artery disease. Xerox has gone public with the fact that it costs it roughly $1.5 million to replace a top executive struck down prematurely by a coronary ailment.

Wellness programs include not only smoke cessation but also fitness, exercise, stress management, diet and weight loss, and special programs for identifying symptoms that can lead to lost work hours.

That's what business wants, and if it doesn't get it from local health care providers, it will go elsewhere for the product.

Alcohol and Substance Abuse

One of the fastest rising areas in which hospitals are becoming involved is onsite alcohol and substance abuse centers. The facilities are in place, the beds are there, and the staff is on board. In fact, now that drinking and drugs have come out of the social closet, admitting to a problem and seeking treatment have almost become chic.

HMOs and PPOs

Here is another fast-growing field. Statistics show that enrollment in HMOs increased 21.2 percent in the period June 1983-June 1984. Currently, there are more than 16 million enrollees in 300-plus plans nationwide. The story of preferred provider organizations (PPOs) is just as spectacular. The American Hospital Association reported only 35 operational PPOs in 1983; two years later, the number had swelled to 115. It should be obvious that these two cousins are not a fad and show strong growth and opportunity potential for hospitals.

Multihospital Systems

In the late 1970s the proprietary hospital chains showed the not-for-profits new ways to manage and market. Proprietary hospitals went out and bought "mom and pop" hospitals. By 1982, the situation was a little different. Hospitals no longer wanted to be bought. In 1982, 33.8 percent of all nonfederal, community hospitals were either owned, leased, or managed by a system and the growth trend to multihospital groups continued. Among the different types of systems, the most significant growth (75.7 percent) occurred in the not-for-profit field. Continued growth was expected as hospitals sought management expertise in the changing health care environment. Teaching and public hospitals were expected to turn increasingly to the option of affiliating with a multihospital system. Therein lie the seeds of opportunity for joint ventures as well.

RED FLAGS

- Make sure your hospital is geared to change before you embark on the joint venture journey.
- Be clear that you have a good working relationship with your medical staff. A joint venture that goes sour can do severe damage to the relationship between hospital and physicians.
- Take your time. Don't jump on the joint venture bandwagon just because everyone else is doing it.

WRAP-UP

The atmosphere is thick with confusion—the very best time for aggressive and forward-thinking hospital administrators to take hold and develop new opportunities and joint ventures for their institutions. To paraphrase an old academic adage—venture or perish.

CHECKLIST

Know what business you are really in and write it down:

Identify the top products you have in your hospital:

1.

2.

3.

4.

5.

Determine the needs of the patients in your market sphere:

1.

2.

3.

4.

5.

6.

7.

8.

9.

10.

Define the unique demographics that have an impact on your facility:

List your organizational strengths and weaknesses in the following areas:

1. Marketing:
2. Advertising:
3. Planning:
4. Finance:
5. Sales:
6. Product Development

List information to be gathered in the following areas:

1. New Patients:
2. Corporate Reorganization:
3. Social and Demographic:
4. Outpatient:
5. Satellites:
6. Programs:
7. Joint Ventures:

Identify areas to be explored for new product development in the following opportunity fields:

1. Hotel Hospital:
2. Aging of America:
3. Nursing Homes:
4. Quality-of-life campuses:
5. Home health services:
6. Mental Illness:
7. HMO and PPO:
8. Alcohol and substance abuse:
9. Multihospital systems:

Develop a timetable for research, decision making, and implementation:

Chapter 2

Benefits for Hospitals

THE WORLD HAS A WAY OF GIVING WHAT IS DEMANDED OF IT. IF YOU ARE FRIGHTENED AND LOOK FOR FAILURE AND POVERTY, YOU WILL GET THEM NO MATTER HOW HARD YOU MAY TRY TO SUCCEED. LACK OF FAITH IN YOURSELF, IN WHAT LIFE WILL DO FOR YOU, CUTS YOU OFF FROM THE GOOD THINGS OF THE WORLD. EXPECT VICTORY AND YOU MAKE VICTORY. NOWHERE IS THIS TRUER THAN IN BUSINESS LIFE, WHERE BRAVERY AND FAITH BRING BOTH MATERIAL AND SPIRITUAL REWARDS.

Preston Bradley

WHAT WE SEE DEPENDS MAINLY ON WHAT WE LOOK FOR.

John Lubbock

HIGHLIGHTS

- Competition
- Financial Returns
- Influences and Control
- The Entrepreneurial Factor
- Marketing Benefits
- Critical Factors To Consider
- Expanding Existing Hospital Markets
- Physician-Related Benefits
- Strategic Planning Benefits
- Financial Benefits
- Operational Benefits

2

WELCOME TO A WHOLE NEW SEASON

Joint ventures are a whole new ball game. The teams are still being picked—there's lots of trading going on. The stands are packed with spectators waiting to see how it all comes out. The proponents are busy selling the benefits, not unlike stadium vendors yelling, "Get your red-hots." The naysayers are complaining that the bubbles will evaporate, like the fizz in a bottle of beer on a warm baseball afternoon.

JOINT VENTURES: THE *BUSINESS* OF MEDICINE

It used to be, back in the good old days of five or so years ago that hospitals and doctors provided a service to patients. Today, there are few in the health care field who could ignore the business aspect that has not just crept into the field but has roared through it like a flood of lava rushing down the side of a volcano. Whatever stands in its path is obliterated, and the landscape never looks the same again. But, unlike the dead soil left after a volcanic eruption, the joint venture eruption is coating the health care field with a rich, fertile loam—a terrific breeding ground for new opportunities.

With the advent of joint ventures, health care came of age. Now it is playing with the boys of business in the big leagues. This business component has come not a moment too soon. Had the health care industry not made a 360-degree revolution and begun to see itself as business, it could well have suffered irrevocable losses and complications. As it is, by taking a corporate view through joint ventures, health care has opened up new benefits for all its players.

BENEFITS OF JOINT VENTURES

Competition

There is no question that since the mid-1970s there have been major shifts in the competitive structure of health care components. Formerly, hospitals served their local communities, the giant teaching hospitals acting as anchors for state-of-the-art surgical procedures, research, and education. If there was competition among local hospitals, it was friendly, the sparring of equally matched partners who knew that after the round they would hit the showers together, refreshed by their workout.

Competition was for the star doctors, the bright young students, maybe even for the mothers in a new development or subdivision. But competition alone would not have shifted the patient universe. Everyone still would maintain their slice of the patient pie.

> Not anymore.

Suddenly competition became a fight for survival itself. It stopped being friendly. Hospitals competed hard, gobbling up the slices of the patient pie from each other. They competed with their own physicians pulling more and more services away from private practitioners in an effort to hold onto market share and, if not to increase their revenue base, at least not to erode it. The situation was tense. There were only so many patients and suddenly they had lots of health care options.

Then came the joint venture. It is to the credit of the health care profession that joint ventures were conceived, born, and now are flourishing. While competition still is fierce, joint ventures took the edge off. Competition now is constructive rather than destructive and the industry can grow competitively just like any other major business in America.

> You have a shilling. I have a shilling. We swap. You have my shilling and I have yours. We are no better off. But suppose you have an idea and I have an idea. We swap. Now you have two ideas and I have two ideas. We have increased our stock of ideas by 100 percent.
>
> *A.S. Gregg*

Financial Returns

> It has been said that money never starts an idea; it is the idea that starts the money.

Let's be realistic. Joint ventures wouldn't be popular at all if there wasn't a good chance that they would be financially rewarding. Many are—most, in fact. Joint ventures provide infusions of large doses of capital into a tired industry, like a deep breath of pure oxygen for the marathon runner with two miles to go before the finish line. By cooperating with physicians, other hospitals, and other corporations, the hospital that participates in joint ventures is involved in a business synergy in which the whole often is greater than the sum of its parts.

By setting up joint ventures, the hospital acquires access to large amounts of capital that it would be hard-pressed to raise on its own from conservative, reluctant donors. This capital then allows the hospital and its joint-venture partners to invest in megabucks high-tech equipment such as MRIs, build free-standing ambulatory care clinics, construct condominium professional offices, and, most importantly, to grow.

Influence and Control

Joint ventures provide opportunities for the health care industry to exercise control over the costs and the quality of services being offered.

> As it is, many outside forces—government, business, alternative delivery systems—are pressing to control and influence the costs of medicine. With co-venturing, the health care industry has a greater opportunity to call the shots.

The Entrepreneurial Factor

Not to be discounted is the excitement of the entrepreneurialism inherent in joint ventures. There is the stimulation of risk and the hope of reward. There is the research, the stretching of business minds and resources, the interaction with completely new players, and the surprise of dealing with old partners in very different ways.

Entreneurialism, while bringing with it tension and fear, also is basic to American business. With the advent of joint ventures, hospitals have become key players—the most recent and most full of potential—in any generation of entrepreneurs.

From General to Specific

In a mid-1980s study, a majority of the hospitals polled reported their reasons for joint venturing: 37 percent to increase market share, 20 percent to lock in utilization, and 13 percent to improve their competitive position. Those are the general benefits of joint venturing. There also are specific ones for hospitals taking that first, second, or even third leap into the joint-venture arena.

MARKETING BENEFITS

The benefits comprising marketing include the protection of hospital markets, their expansion, and the gaining of other marketing advantages.

Protection of Hospital Markets

By entering into joint ventures, hospitals protect their markets through horizontal integration. For example, by linking with other health care providers such as other hospitals, long-term care facilities, and multi-hospital systems they in a sense are guaranteeing that their market share will not be invaded by other, aggressive seekers of new patients and that potential competitors will not encroach on their patient territory.

Hospitals also protect their markets through vertical integration: for example, they can consolidate with different types of providers covering a range of services from nursing homes, to ambulatory care centers, to housing. In this way, hospitals make their presence felt in medical and medically related services, having a place into which to feed their patients, without losing them permanently from their sphere of influence and financial control, and in return receiving an influx of new patients from the joint-venture partner that may have been tempted to expand services or send patients to other institutions.

Integration through joint ventures can lead to cost savings. If patients can be served more efficiently and if hospital costs can be curbed, the savings can be passed on to the patient universe. Hence, hospitals joint venturing with various suppliers, manufacturers, and distributors on buying in bulk can produce considerable savings. An example of this joint venture to economize and, through economies of scale, protect the patient base is the reported agreement between a major hospital chain and a single distributor of medical and surgical supplies that could save the hospital $4 million annually.

What are the critical factors in protecting market share?

> What are the critical factors in protecting market share?
>
> - Hospitals must consider the level and degree of commitment of the partners: Who has the most to gain? Are benefits and risks equally balanced?
> - Hospitals must determine the overall scope of participation and involvement. Keep in mind that nothing ruins a partnership faster than one partner is beginning to get the niggling doubt that it somehow is getting the short end of the stick.
> - Both partners must make sure their missions are similar. Conflict arises when the cultures of the two partners do not mesh. Examine the basic philosophy critically so that there will not be hostility later.
> - Both partners must integrate financial and business plans and objectives. A joint venture falls apart quickly if the financial expectations of both parties are poles apart.
> - Both partners must be sure product and service mix already in place for each one's patient universe is compatible. Like oil and water, hospitals are very different in what they offer and thus may not make the best partners in securing each other's already precarious market share.

Expansion of Existing Markets

Another marketing benefit is the ability for the joint venture to expand the hospitals' market base. One way is through the development of alternative delivery systems (ADS). For some time, the health insurance market has been shifting from indemnity insurance to ADS or prepaid health plans. These fall into two main categories: the HMO and the PPO. Their key to success is the integration of financing and delivery of health care with the resultant increase in control of overall costs.

These ADS offer a strong marketing benefit for hospitals. It has been estimated that by 1990, total HMO enrollment will top the 30 million mark. That is 14 percent of the total population and 7 percent of the market. Better yet, industry analysts predict an annual growth rate of 20 percent for HMO industry and PPOS are not far behind in growth and numbers.

Think of the possibilities for hospitals to entertain entire universes of patients that previously were closed and now are guaranteed.

What are the critical factors to consider in alternative delivery systems?

- The partners must recognize that alternative delivery systems are fast becoming one of the basic ways to offer health care services to almost any patient universe.
- Hospitals must investigate thoroughly their patient universes, their need for alternative delivery systems, and their relationship with any alternative delivery system that is developed.
- Hospitals must recognize that they will need to hire professionals skilled in the alternative delivery system who will be able to communicate with that model effectively.
- Hospitals must develop the ability to negotiate aggressively with ADS to retain market share.
- The partners must develop increased data management systems for constant monitoring and updating of payment arrangements.

PHYSICIAN-RELATED BENEFITS

There are strong benefits for physicians in forming cooperative joint ventures. Let's look at what is happening to practitioners in this time of change in the health care field. For them, it could be said that it never rains, but it pours. Times were when a medical license was virtually a guarantee of status in the community, economic security, prestige, freedom to practice anywhere in the country—in short, all good things would come to those who completed medical school.

> Times have changed, and the physicians who survive and thrive in this climate are the ones who look on their glass of opportunity as being half-full, rather than half-empty.

Studies show that the growth of medical care resources has been so rapid as to overtake the growth of the U.S. population. In the decade between 1970 and 1980, the number of physicians increased 40 percent and is projected by analysts to grow by more than 50 percent between 1980 and 2000. Coupled with this is the fact that the number of hospital beds per active physician fell from 5.2 in 1970 to 3.1 in 1980.

To further complicate the situation for physicians, the number of allied health professionals has risen dramatically: 136 percent for active physician assistants and 39 percent for registered nurses. This in part has had a negative impact on the income of physicians, which has dropped (factoring in inflation) by 0.7 percent in the ten years from 1973 to 1983. "Increases in physician net income have lagged behind inflation for most of the past decade, decreasing purchasing power at an average rate of 0.8 percent a year" (*Medical Economics,* March 31, 1986). It is also noted that aggregate physician spending power will decline at twice that rate during the next decade. After a correction for inflation, real physician income will drop from $102,000 in 1984 to about $85,000 in 1995. By 1995, only about one percent of physicians will earn more than $200,000.

All these factors offer physicians and hospitals opportunities and benefits to enter joint ventures since both are in essentially the same patient crunch.

> What are the critical factors to consider in forming physician-related joint ventures?
>
> - Both hospitals and physicians must reconsider their relationship and recognize that success for both is linked to their ability to integrate their needs and abilities successfully.
> - Hospitals must recognize that as physicians become business partners, they demand and deserve greater management responsibilities in such areas as strategic planning, recruitment of other doctors, budget development, and utilizations of quality control.
> - Both physicians and hospitals must guarantee

performance at fixed prices to patients, industry, alternative delivery systems, and payers.

- Hospitals must be prepared to enhance the practices of their physician partners by providing access to capital, to marketing and management expertise, and to a supply of joint ventures to ensure a healthy partnership.
- Hospitals will have to research the professional and business needs of their physician-partners. This could take the form of leveraging physician practices, focus groups with clinic managers, and joint attendance at seminars and educational forums.
- Hospitals must become willing to explore creative legal and organizational arrangements for relating in a corporate sense to their physician-partners.
- Hospitals must develop a trust relationship with physicians and take a more active leadership role, acting the part of risk-takers in these new joint ventures.

Overall, the prognosis for physicians and hospitals working together in joint ventures is good. For decades, they have been partners in providing medical care to their patient markets. The difference now is that the opportunities have become expanded beyond the service sector and into the corporate arena. Not a bad deal for either party.

STRATEGIC PLANNING BENEFITS

Among all the benefits accruing to hospitals from this wave of joint venturing, the strategic planning benefits are among the most exciting. No longer can hospitals just rely on their small, discrete, blue H to guarantee a rush, or even a steady trickle, of patients. However through joint ventures hospitals now have the opportunity of flexing their creative clout through exploration of diverse markets and new technologies.

Strategic planning for diversification of health care products opens up new avenues previously left neglected by hospitals. Now they are having to research new possibilities for diversification actively and with a degree of specialization never before needed.

What are the critical factors to be considered in strategic planning?

- The aging of American health care consumers creates new opportunities for hospitals since both the aggregate economic condition of the aged has improved and their numbers have increased significantly and will continue to do so until the turn of the century—seven million more by the year 2000. Strategies for hospitals to explore include ways to reduce the cost of health care to this growing market and the expansion of services such as nursing homes, home health care, HMOs, and housing.
- The veterans market is a neglected area of strategic planning and one that can become significant. It is predicted that as the numbers of veterans grow, the federal government will be looking for ways to shift the burden to the private sector. The opportunity is ripe for creative joint ventures with Veterans Administration (VA), hospitals, and for developing and participating in new forms of insurance coverage for veterans.
- Hospitals should take a close look at changing ethnic patterns. Hispanics are predicted to be the largest minority group in the United States both through birth and immigration by the end of 1985. Next come Asians. There are fresh opportunities for planning programs and services that take into account the varying religious and cultural customs of this new market. Adjustments in staff language skills and the research and treatment of diseases indigenous to a different population should be considered seriously.
- Tremendous opportunities lie in the wellness movement, which does not seem to have exhausted itself, despite the efforts of such influences as the Jane Fonda tapes, diet books ad nauseum, and the death of James Fixx, the patron saint of joggers.
- Hospitals will have to look beyond the treatment of the sick and study opportunities for attracting the well.

FINANCIAL BENEFITS

It has been said that finance is the art of passing money from one hand to the other, until it disappears.

Not so. In fact, it could be said that in joint ventures in health care, finance is the art of passing money from one hand to the other until it grows and multiplies severalfold. For of course it is the financial consideration—the incredibly high risks and the equally high rewards—that make joint ventures in health care such an exhilarating prospect.

Benefits in the financial component

1. It enables the partners to share the financial risks inherent in new or start-up businesses.
2. It reduces the individual partner's cost of investing in the new venture.
3. It makes it easier to attract outside equity capital.

Here's how these three benefits break out under analysis.

Realities To Be Confronted

Look at the various realities facing hospitals today.

They have changing capital needs.

They need to locate sources of capital to renovate and replace outmoded facilities and to expand capacity to meet demand, particularly in certain demographically fast growing areas of the country (sunbelt states).

They need to keep pace with technological developments—an increasingly expensive proposition as the costs of technology keep escalating into the seven-figure area.

They need to diversify and change their mix in terms of services and markets, a continuing project that takes large amounts of initial capital. These factors are complicated by a growing number of financial constraints.

FINANCIAL CONSTRAINTS

- The diagnosis related group (DRG) program is severely restricting revenues.
- Federal regulatory control of hospitals' revenues has increased through such congressional measures as the Tax Equity and Fiscal Responsibility Act (TEFRA) and the Medicare Prospective Payment System (PPS).

- Third party payers are putting on pressure in an attempt to reduce their share.
- Greater competition for donors dollars is putting the squeeze on hospitals' ability to maintain their fund-raising dollars.
- Hospitals are becoming increasingly dependent on the debt market to finance their capital projects.
- The debt market in turn is beginning to view hospitals as increasingly risky. A point of proof: DRGs.
- Health care is a political issue.

Take a look at the hospital under fiscal stress. Reliable economic sources predict that there will be significant capital shortfalls—in excess of $50 billion—by 1990. Hospitals that are most likely to be hit by this shortfall and that will have trouble accessing fresh sources of capital will be characterized by the following.

- High Medicare and Medicaid utilization
- High bad-debt expense
- Declining or extremely competitive market
- Obsolete buildings and facilities
- Aging, unreliable, tired equipment
- Poorer quality medical staff
- High debt-equity ratios
- Noncompetitive price structures.

Where Do We Go from Here?

What does all this spell out? To observant, shrewd, and financially astute hospital administrators these trends and events clearly mean a cooperative effort in obtaining financing through joint ventures rather than relying on old, less reliable sources of funds. When this fiscal bulb lights up, realistic hospital administrators will recognize the following factors as positives, or at least as potential positives, for their own facilities.

- New sources of funds will become available through reorganization, restructuring, service diversification, and marketing strategies. It stands to reason: The more a hospital has to offer, the more attractive it becomes from a financial point of view.

- Hospitals will become more careful, spending more time and analysis on cost/benefit types of decisions. This will improve their business acumen greatly, and with it their ability to profit from the money crisis.
- Hospitals will become more creative in finding and developing new products, making them more attractive to business partners who constantly are seeking greater penetration into the consumer market.
- Innovative challenges will have to be met in the delivery of high quality health care for less money. Not a bad thing, since here as in all areas the old saying holds true, "Necessity is the mother of invention." Who is to say that the shortage of cash and the influx of new partners won't be a good thing in the long run.

> There is an old saying in business: Invest with OPM (other people's money).

Not a bad rule to follow, and joint venturing for the first time permits the hospital to indulge in that formerly rare luxury. Look at how it was before. Hospitals invested heavily in bricks and mortar to build a facility for their medical staff. They invested in technology. They invested in equipment. They invested in R&D. All this investment on the part of hospitals and they invested alone . . . with their own capital.

Now look how joint ventures have changed the investment pattern. Physicians—both internal medical staffs and outside groups—are putting in cash. Venture capitalists, other corporate structures, banks, suppliers, manufacturers . . . the list goes on and on and on. And what is the bottom line? Hospitals are finding partners to share the risk and to act as a form of fiscal insurance. Remember that business partners like to make money, not lose it. So the reassurance factor for hospitals has increased.

ATTRACTING EQUITY CAPITAL

While it is not a guarantee, financial trends point to the fact that hospitals will be able to continue to find and place capital into their projects. However, there are threats to this capital pool that administrators should be aware of.

- Possible elimination of tax exempt financing
- Limits on philanthropic incentive
- Elimination of industrial revenue bonds and their cap
- Medicare/PPS treatment of capital costs

However, there is a response to these threats and some hospitals have taken positive steps in ensuring their access to outside capital:

- Hospitals have begun to assume less fixed-rate, long-term debt.
- Hospitals are looking at more short-term debt and commercial paper for working capital and short-lived assets.
- Hospitals are looking at a variable debt rate.
- Hospitals are using insurance as a credit enhancement.
- Hospital joint ventures are a reality.
- Hospitals are seeking intermediate term debt for equipment loan pools.

Critical factors in analyzing financial benefits

- Free-standing and less stable institutions will have less access to capital and at higher cost.
- Systems, groups, and insured hospital issues will account for the majority of applicants for credit.
- Hospitals will find it necessary to divest themselves of nonperforming assets to refocus operating funds.
- A hard look will have to be taken at joint ventures between not-for-profit and for-profit companies to leverage capital.

OPERATIONAL BENEFITS

An acre of performance is worth a whole world of promise.

William Dean Howells

And here is the true test of the new arrangement: the joint venture. Performance is so closely tied in to the other benefits that it is perhaps the single most important factor to consider. As with every important change, there are significant benefits accruing to hospitals that translate performance into creative operational benefits.

Operational Benefit # 1: Obtaining Needed Skills

The hospital industry is having to look at itself the way other product and service industries have looked at themselves since the beginning of business. In the past the hospital market was restricted to physicians and patients. Today, markets are opening up in other areas such as physician groups, employers, insurers, and HMOs/PPOs. These new markets are underscoring with a double line the need for new operational skills that, if developed and nurtured, will reap benefits to the hospital.

Look at what opportunities and benefits are forthcoming to hospitals in the new health care climate. If developed, they will significantly alter the operation of the traditional hospital forever.

- *Market Research:* Analyzing demographics, conducting attitude surveys, and identifying needs and expectations.
- *Product Development:* Repackaging tired old products and creating vibrant new ones.
- *Pricing:* Developing pricing policies that keep hospitals competitive; gone are the days when pricing was haphazard.
- *Staff Training:* Providing employees with nontechnical skills and helping them beef up their people skills, now more important than ever.
- *Advertising:* Organizing advertising departments to communicate the products and services the hospitals offer to the patient universe.
- *Public Relations:* developing new strategies to communicate effectively and profitably with new and old constituencies alike.
- *Sales:* Establishing entire new levels of skills, and departments to implement and monitor those skills—something unheard of in the past.
- *Marketing:* Developing and keeping a solid market share in the economy, a need that has created an entirely new operations perception for many hospitals that used to pooh-pooh the crassness of marketing efforts in other industries.

Operational Benefit # 2: Cost Effectiveness

One of the critical areas of which every health care administrator is painfully aware is the pressure on hospitals to contain costs. While at first this seems like forcing blood from a hospital stone that already has a dwindling supply, it is a great if somewhat hidden opportunity.

Examine the grim statistics and trends (statistics taken from *Philadelphia Inquirer,* July 30, 1986, 315(30): 1-A, 8-A).

- Health care expenditures decreased nationally from 11.7 percent in 1978 to 10.3 percent in 1983.
- Spending for health care in 1985 increased to a record $425 billion—an 8.9 percent increase over 1984 $390.2 billion.
- Spending for hospital services increased 5.5 percent in 1985. Hospital expenditures were $166 billion—40 percent of health care spending.
- Cost-per-case was $1721 per person in 1985—up from $1595 in 1984.

What are the benefits of these numbers to hospitals?

1. Hospitals must screen expenses and capital investments more carefully and try to match them to increased staff productivity.
2. Hospitals must develop a higher degree of financial sophistication in capital allocation.
3. Hospitals must shop carefully to capitalize on the best possible prices—an approach that will become the norm rather than the exception.
4. Hospitals must make investments in productivity research and management information systems for cost control.
5. Hospitals must develop risk management and reinsurance pools for growing professional and product liability risks.

Operational Benefit # 3: Economies of Scale

Like their corporate brothers, hospitals must develop economies of scale. Negotiations with suppliers will have to change. Tough new guidelines and pressures will be brought to bear on supplier industries to share the price crunch with hospitals.

Hospitals will form alliances for improved purchasing power of all supplies from towels and surgical instruments to services such as consulting skills to reduce the costs.

Such cost reduction methods will create their own unique joint venture bonds.

WRAP-UP

Exciting, fresh, stimulating benefits await hospitals that take the risk in joint ventures in the late 1980s and early 1990s. Expanded markets, a cooperative relationship with physicians, widened horizons in strategic planning and development, profit and increased revenues, and, finally, new departments and systems to serve expanded patient universes and market new products all are on the horizon.

But these will be there only for hospital administrators who see the mid-1980s situation of flux as one of opportunity to stretch their own and their organizations' resources to new levels of fitness and health through joint ventures.

> RED FLAGS
>
> - Be careful to use the competitive environment in a positive, not negative, way.
> - Keep your own bottom line firmly in mind.
> - Don't give away too much just to do the deal.
> - You can't be all things to all people; make sure your priorities are clear.
> - Make sure the joint venture is a good fit for your hospital first and foremost.
> - Watch for disgruntled staff members on your newly revamped joint venture organization chart.

CHECKLIST

MARKETING BENEFITS

List three different marketing benefits you could achieve for your hospital through joint ventures:

1. ____

2. ____

3. ____

List critical areas of concern that you would need to research and control to best take advantage of the marketing benefits:

____

____

____

PHYSICIAN BENEFITS

Take a fresh look at your physicians as a business resource or partner. What do they bring into the business?

1. ____

2. ____

3. ____

Look at your hospital vis-à-vis the physicians and list what it brings to the table in a joint venture:

1. ____

2. ____

3. ____

STRATEGIC PLANNING

List five strategies, never before employed by you or your hospital, to enhance a joint venture:

1. ____

2. ____

3. ______________________________

4. ______________________________

5. ______________________________

FINANCIAL BENEFITS

List five new, fresh sources of capital:

Source 1: ______________________________

Source 2: ______________________________

Source 3: ______________________________

Source 4: ______________________________

Source 5: ______________________________

Now, just as you think you have exhausted every source for new capital, list two more:

Source 6: ______________________________

Source 7: ______________________________

OPERATIONAL BENEFITS

Redraw your hospital organizational chart to include such areas as marketing, strategic planning, acquisitions and divestitures, advertising, public relations, patient/guest relations, R&D, long-range planning, and development.

Chapter 3

Finding Joint Venture Partners

WHAT NEEDS TO BE CULTIVATED AMONG MEN INTERESTED IN SOCIAL RELATIONSHIPS WHETHER AS OWNER, MANAGER, OR EMPLOYEE; PRODUCER OR CONSUMER; SELLER OR BUYER; PARTNER OR COMPETITOR; IS SELF-CONTROL. REFRAINING FROM UNFAIR ADVANTAGE, DETERMINATION TO GIVE FAIR VALUE AS WELL AS TO TAKE IT; THE APPRECIATION THAT IMMEDIATE GAIN IS NOT THE PRINCIPAL CONSIDERATION; THAT ONE GROUP CANNOT CONTINUE TO PROFIT AT THE EXPENSE OF ANOTHER WITHOUT EVENTUAL LOSS TO BOTH; THAT ALL CLASSES OF MEN ARE MUTUALLY DEPENDENT ON THE SERVICES OF EACH OTHER; THAT THE BEST SERVICE YIELDS THE GREATEST PROFIT.

PRESTON S. ARKWRIGHT

HIGHLIGHTS

- Shopping List of Prospective Partners
- Preshopping list Considerations
- Objectives for Joint Venturing with Partners
- Overview of Joint Venture Activity
- The Multies/The Independents
- The Most Popular Choice—Hospitals with Docs
- What's In It for the Doctors
- What's In It for the Hospital
- Types of Joint Ventures with Doctors
- Case Studies in Joint Ventures
- The MeSH: Pros and Cons
- Joint Ventures with Long-Term Care Facilities
- Hospital with Home Health Care
- Teaching Hospitals with For-Profits
- Other Arrangements

3

WHO COULD HOSPITALS JOINT VENTURE WITH? THAT'S THE QUESTION

The joint venture band has struck up. The strains of the joint-venture waltz fill the air. The stag line shifts nervously. Who to dance with? What partner has room on the joint-venture dance card? What promise lingers in the air after the dance is over? How will it all end? A walk back to the stag line or the beginnings of a joint-venture romance?

That's about where potential joint venture partners in health co-ventures are now: Eying each other carefully from across the industry, checking out who is new, who has been around the block before, and who has what to offer. Some find each other and form happy unions; others get together, compare agendas, and realize they are not a perfect, or even close, fit.

So, who to form a joint-venture relationship with remains the key.

The first step is to develop a shopping list of prospective partners.

- Physician groups and hospitals
- Individual physicians and hospitals
- Hospitals and long-term facilities
- Hospitals and home health service companies
- Teaching hospitals and the for-profit hospital industry
- Hospitals with private for-profit corporations
- Hospitals and insurance companies
- Hospitals and HMOs
- HMOs, insurance companies, and multihospitals

PRE-SHOPPING LIST CONSIDERATIONS

Before you go into the joint-venture market with your shopping list of carefully compiled partners, make sure you know exactly what you are shopping for. Examine the objectives carefully. A useful analogy might be to plan the menu before you go shopping for the food. It won't do you any good to buy smoked salmon if you had planned to serve artichoke hearts vinaigrette as an appetizer. Nor will your party succeed if the menu lists rack of lamb and you end up serving dover sole. Both might be equally tasty, but they are very different dishes.

Figure 3-1 points out a number of potential joint-venture partners.

When you do start your shopping for joint venturing, your objectives should be to:

- Acquire new sources of capital
- Increase revenue base
- Achieve economies of scale
- Update technology

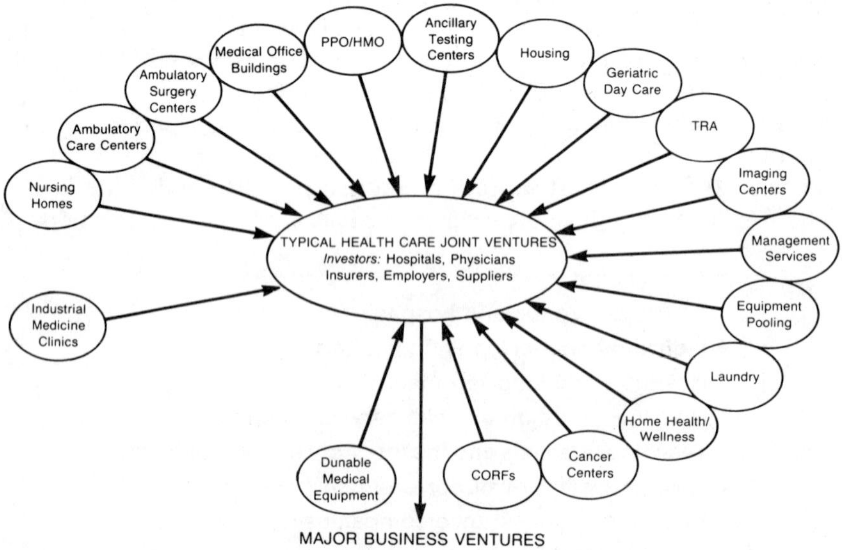

Figure 3-1 Typical Joint Venture Partners Chart

Source: Adapted from *Dimensions in Health Care* with permission of Peat, Marwick, Mitchell and Company, © September 1985.

- Maintain current business practices
- Reduce costs
- Share financial risks and rewards
- Introduce new patient markets
- Increase physician alliances
- Improve productivity
- Provide management expertise
- Increase employer/employee commitment

> **WARNING!!!!!!**
>
> **Don't look to your joint-venture partner to satisfy all the above objectives, but do expect many to be fulfilled. Otherwise, what's the point of co-venturing in the first place? But as in a marriage, one partner can't fulfill all the needs, goals, dreams, and expectations of the other. Be realistic. (See Exhibit 3-1.)**

Exhibit 3-1 Screening Criteria for New Ventures

1. Does the proposal fit within the corporation's organizational mission?
2. What is the return on investment? Initial capital requirement?
3. Does the project have continuing potential or is it a one-shot deal, and does it have other economic spinoffs? Can the spinoffs be quantified or measured?
4. To what extent does the project depend on cost-based reimbursement versus charge-based or on private fee-for-service arrangements?
5. What is the financial profile of the patients/customers likely to utilize the proposed service?
6. Does the proposal require approval by any government agency?
7. Does the proposed project imply any conflict with the interests of the board of directors or medical staff?
8. How portable is the commitment to the project (i.e., can we pull out if it fails)?
9. Is the project legal and ethical and does it affect our image?
10. Is timing a critical factor in the project?
11. What is the impact of this project on management resources and time? Do we have experience and expertise in this area? Is it already available in the community?
12. What is the competition and alternative to the proposed new project or service?
13. What is the need/demand for this service?
14. What is the impact on existing resources and facilities?
15. What is the proposed organizational structure for this new project?

Source: Reprinted from *Profiles in Hospital Marketing,* pp. 14–15, with permission of Wentworth Publishing Company, © October 1984.

OVERVIEW OF JOINT-VENTURE ACTIVITY

In a study by one of the Big Eight accounting firms, interesting facts came to light (Figure 3-2) about joint venture partnering:

- Joint-venture partners of choice by a significant margin were physician group practices. Of hospitals already involved in joint ventures, 40 percent reported that physician groups were their current partners and 48 percent said that physician groups were highest on their list of prospective partners.
- Individual physicians were the second partners of choice listed by 24 percent of hospitals already involved in joint ventures and by 30 percent of hospitals interested.
- Corporations other than health care providers were mentioned as likely partners by 9 percent of the hospitals already involved and by only 7 percent of these interested in co-venturing.
- Co-venturing with home health providers or nursing homes was one of the least sought partnerships. There also was a marked reluctance to venture with long-term or acute-care providers.

The Multis and the Independents

The same study underscores the fact that multihospital systems were much more likely to be involved already in joint ventures with physician groups than were the independent hospitals, 45 percent as compared with 38 percent (Figure 3-3). However, both the multis and the independents showed an extremely positive interest in pursuing physician groups as partners.

The independents were more likely to be involved or interested in ventures with other hospitals (Figure 3-4). Given their existing affiliation, as part of a chain with other short-term hospitals, it was expected that multihospital system participants would be less likely than independents to joint venture with other hospitals. Independents also were moderately involved or interested in venturing with home health companies. Multihospital system participants did not mention these providers at all.

Physician group practices were the number one choice, regardless of hospital size (Table 3-1). This was particularly true for larger hospitals. Fifty percent of hospitals with more than 400 beds were involved already in a joint venture with a group practice. Sixty-five percent of these hospitals were interested in pursuing joint ventures with physician groups.

For individual physicians, there was little distinction as to hospital size

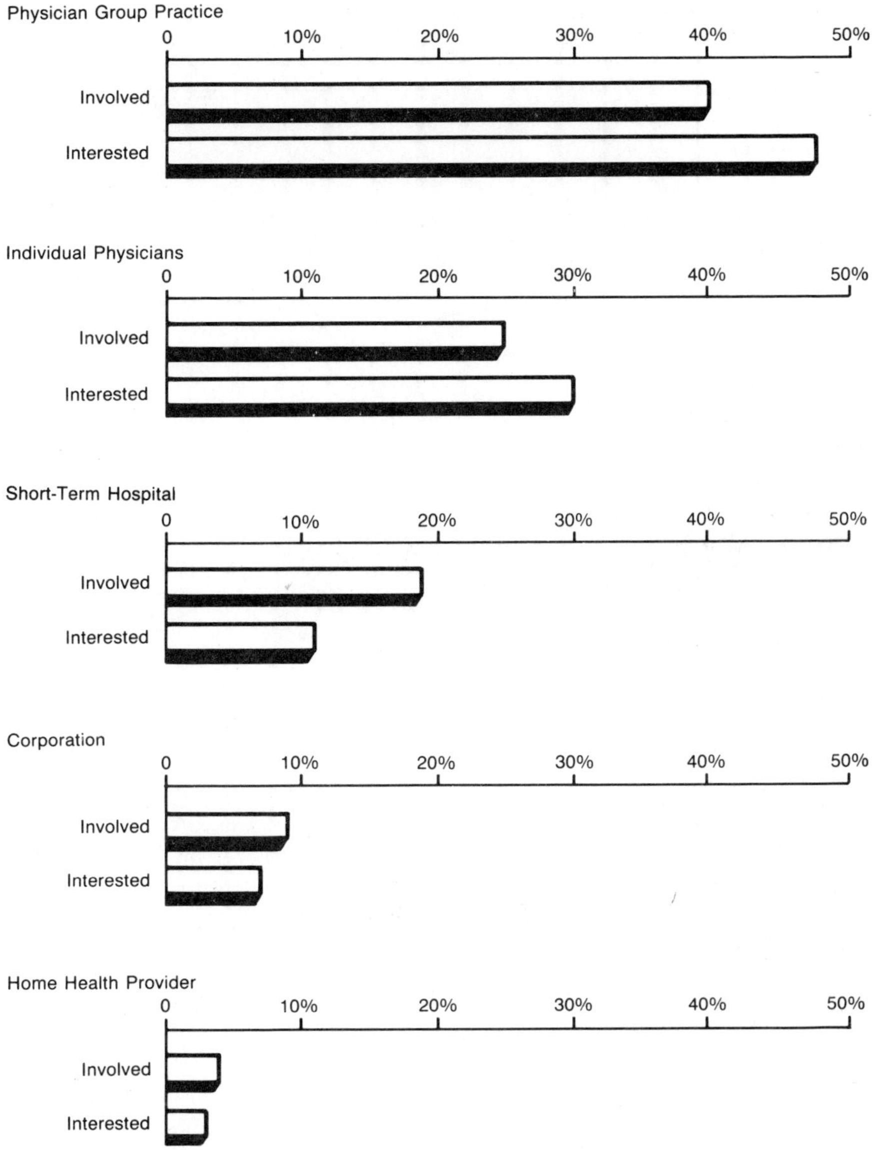

Figure 3-2 Joint-Venture Partners, by Highest Preference

Source: Reprinted from *Health Care Joint Ventures: Survey Results,* p. 27, with permission of Ernst and Whinney, © 1985.

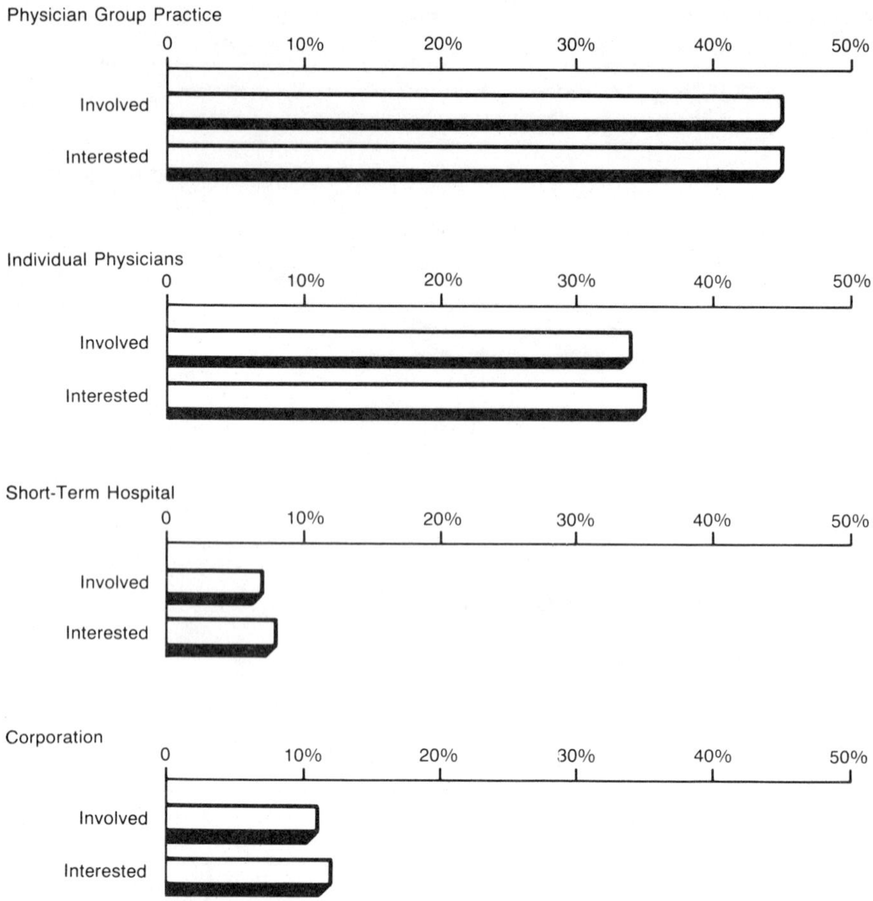

Figure 3-3 Multihospital Systems and Joint-Venture Partners

Source: Reprinted from *Health Care Joint Ventures: Survey Results*, p. 29, with permission of Ernst and Whinney, © 1985.

---

except for those with 100–199 beds. These hospitals were interested in joint venturing with individual physicians 41 percent of the time—a considerably higher percentage than the other groups.

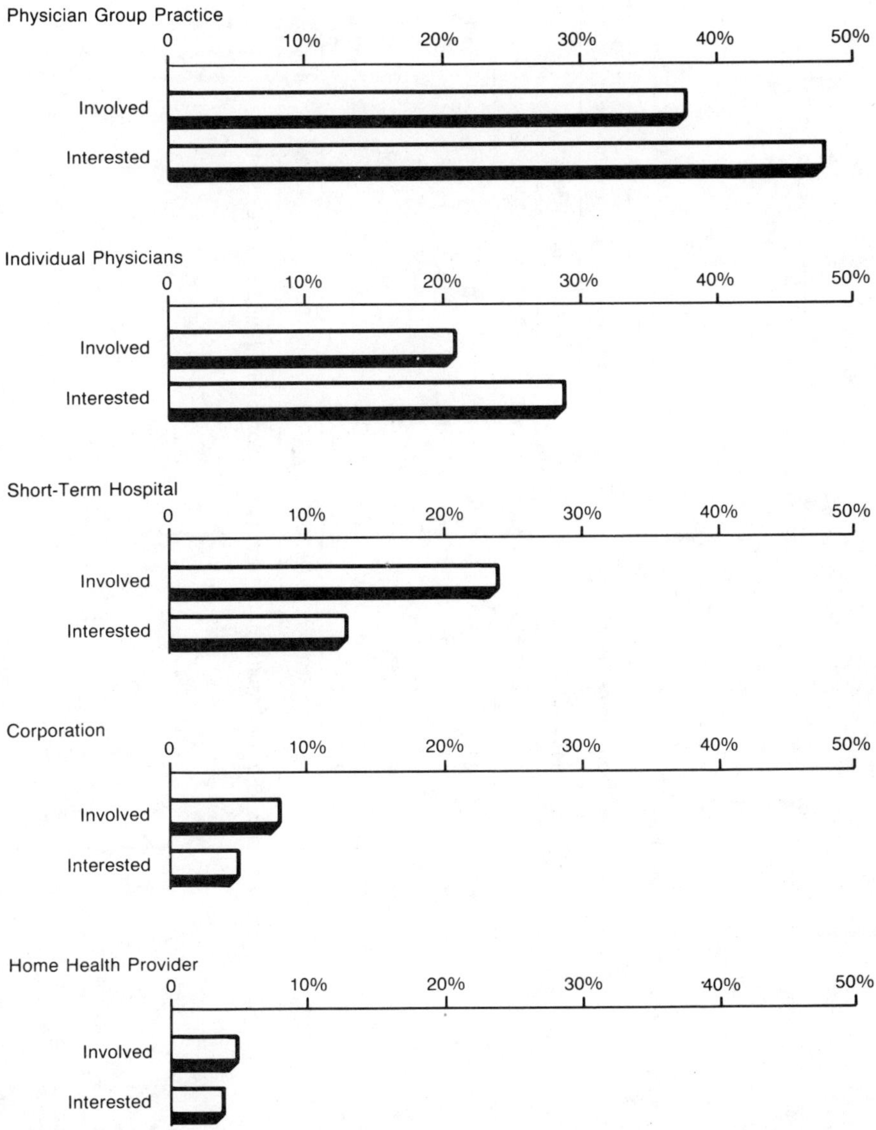

Figure 3-4 Independent Hospitals and Joint-Venture Partners

Source: Reprinted from *Health Care Joint Ventures: Survey Results*, p. 30, with permission of Ernst and Whinney, © 1985.

Table 3-1 Joint-Venture Partners by Size of Hospital

	Involved in Joint Ventures				Interested in Joint Ventures			
	Number of Beds				Number of Beds			
	<100	*100–199*	*200–399*	*>400*	*<100*	*100–199*	*200–399*	*>400*
Group practice	34%	36%	41%	50%	46%	41%	51%	65%
Individual physicians	29	24	21	26	24	41	28	25
Short-term hospital	21	26	16	12	16	9	11	5
Corporation	5	5	11	10	10	3	8	0
Home health provider	3	2	6	2	4	3	2	0
Other answers	8	7	5	0	0	3	0	5
	100%	100%	100%	100%	100%	100%	100%	100%

Source: Reprinted from *Health Care Joint Ventures: Survey Results,* p. 31, with permission of Ernst and Whinney, © 1985.

PICKING THE BEST PARTNER OF THE CROP

> As the gardener, by severe pruning, forces the sap of the tree into one or two vigorous limbs, so should you stop off your miscellaneous activity and concentrate your force on one or a few points.
>
> *Ralph Waldo Emerson*

Good advice. And advice that is particularly suited to the interaction between hospitals and their joint-venture partnering possibilities. (For details on the growth of such ventures, see Figure 3-5.)

Most Popular: Hospitals with Docs

Let's look at joint ventures from the physicians' point of view. As a result of the doctor glut, the proliferation of HMOs and PPOs, and pressure from government and business to contain health care costs, physicians are finding that they no longer can operate as independent professionals in an industry vacuum.

Statistics, from the docs' point of view, look grim: On average physicians are seeing 28 fewer patients a week than they did 10 years ago, with a corresponding drop in their net income. Hospital stays are declining, with patients being released sooner or choosing the ambulatory surgery alternative and bypassing the inpatient role altogether. Doctors are finding it a cold, cruel world out there and are changing their traditional, more adversarial relationship with hospitals in an effort to survive.

What's in It for the Doctors

In fact, doctors and hospitals are natural allies, so by working together, both can survive and prosper, pooling their resources for mutual benefit. Although a financial perk is inherent in joint venturing, the reality is that doctors are amenable to co-venturing as a way to protect their shrinking market share and fiscal base in the health care industry.

What's in It for the Hospitals

Hospitals working in joint ventures with doctors have certain clear advantages.

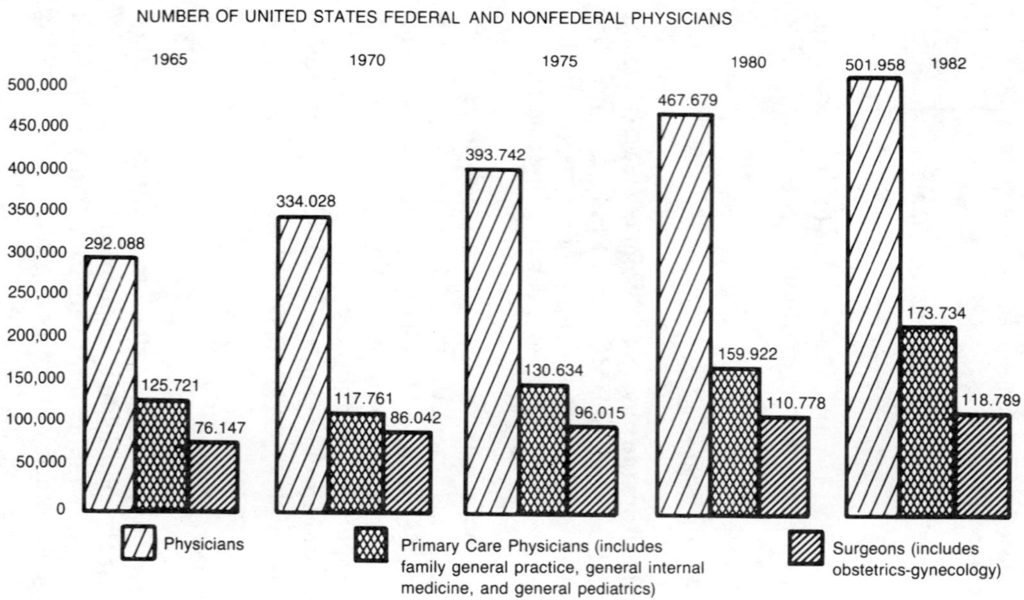

Figure 3-5 Hospital-Physician Ventures: Staffing

Note 1: 1965 data are not entirely comparable with other years presented because of a new classification system initiated in 1968. The new system is based on more functional categories of hours worked in a typical week. The previous system was based or the financial characteristics of a physician's practice.

Note 2: In 1982, of the 501.958 physicians, 64.247 were women, 107.284 were foreign medical graduates; and 19.480 were federally employed.

Sources: Physician Distribution and Medical Licensure in the U.S. (selected years). Chicago: American Medical Association. Physician Characteristics and Distribution in the U.S., 1983 ed. Chicago: American Medical Association.

Source: Reprinted from *Socio-Economic Fact Book for Surgery*, p. 14, with permission of the American College of Surgeons, © 1985.

> - The two are working with a known factor (granted that it is in a new relationship), but hospitals and doctors have been co-workers for decades and have developed a certain understanding of each other's quirks and peculiarities.
> - Physicians can provide the hospital with the necessary staffing and skills to run some of the spinoff ventures that need highly qualified technical expertise.
> - Doctors can provide a large lump of capital input into a venture that might be financially too large for the hospital to swallow on its own.

While there are other "in it's," depending on the particular style and configuration of the venture, by and large these are the major reasons why the hospital-doctor partnership is so popular.

> For most hospitals and doctors, it is really a case of "better the devil you know than one you don't."

Types of Joint Ventures with Physicians

Just as physicians are the preferred partners for many joint ventures, there also are specific hospital–physician joint ventures that work better than others.

> AMBULATORY CARE
>
> 1. ambulatory care centers
> 2. surgery centers
> 3. urgent care centers
> 4. magnetic imaging diagnostic centers
> 5. other diagnostic facilities
>
> ALTERNATIVE DELIVERY SYSTEMS
>
> 1. HMOs
> 2. PPOs
> 3. medical office buildings
> 4. laundry facilities
> 5. long-term or subacute care programs

CASE STUDIES IN JOINT VENTURES WITH DOCTORS

Case # 1

A Midwestern hospital formed a joint venture with its medical staff to combat competition from HMOs and PPOs encroaching in the area. The objectives of the physicians were simple: to keep practicing in their own offices, to keep their current base of patients, and to capture some of the newly opened prepaid market.

How It Works

The joint venture organized a group of physicians from the hospital medical staff under a for-profit holding company. The hospital and the doctors each purchased 50 percent of the stock in the new company. The new company then was in a position to negotiate contracts and to provide services to open panel HMOs and PPOs.

The Results

Half the medical staff bought into the new company and agreed to provide care to PPO and HMO members at a capitated rate. As of mid-1986, one HMO had been signed and more were under negotiation. The goal: to bring in 200,000 new patients between 1986 and 1991.

Case Study # 2

An East Coast hospital wanted to stop other prepaid plans from coming into its immediate market area. To achieve this, it turned to its medical staff for help.

How It Works

The hospital set up a MeSH (*Me*dical *S*taff *H*ospital), which is a unique model of joint ventures between hospitals and their medical staffs (more on the MeSH and how it works later in this chapter). Each participating doctor contributed $500 to the kitty. A holding company was formed that could spin off any number of subsidiaries and the doctors involved could select which of the subsidiary ventures they would become involved with financially.

The Results

While the results weren't all in yet (as with all joint ventures, this was so new that accurate evaluation was not possible), but this particular format seems to suit everyone involved well and offers a real potential of financial gain.

Case Study # 3

On the West Coast, four hospitals and their medical staffs formed a corporation to develop a PPO. In an attempt to offer consumers the kind of health care they wanted at the cost that industry was pressuring local providers to set, this group decided that the best solution was to form its own PPO. Neither hospitals nor independent doctors alone had the clout, or necessary resources, to fill the PPO needs. Together, however they had a good shot.

How It Works

The PPO board consists half of physicians and half of hospital administration and board members. Each participating physician pays in $250 and has the right to select the contracts that doctor signs, giving the individual flexibility in finding just the right fee schedule that meets the need.

The Results

While the numbers were not in yet, the joint venture enabled both the hospitals and the doctors to compete effectively in the new health care climate, where individually they would have been dead in the water.

THE CARDIAC CATH LAB AS A JOINT VENTURE*

Why a Cath Lab?

Hospitals looking for joint venture opportunities with their physicians should consider an outpatient cardiac catheterization laboratory. Although not very price-sensitive yet, outpatient diagnostic cardiac caths can reduce costs by $300 to $600 per procedure, can increase patient convenience and satisfaction, and can increase availability of inpatient facilities. An outpatient diagnostic facility can be a valuable element of the hospital's overall competitive strategy for heart and cardiac services. A

---

*Reprinted from "Joint Venturing Your Outpatient Cardiac Cath Lab" in *Hospital Entrepreneurs Newsletter,* Vol. 1, No. 7, pp. 3, 6–8, Aspen Publishers, Inc., © 1985.

price-competitive outpatient cath lab can be packaged with other cardiovascular procedures and surgeries to provide an edge in negotiating with HMOs and PPOs. Whether you are looking for an economic joint venture with your cardiologists or are looking to expand your cardiac market share, an outpatient cath lab makes good sense.

What Should Be Offered in the Cath Lab

Inpatient cardiac caths have been performed for over 20 years, but outpatient cath labs are a relatively new activity. Diagnostic cardiac caths should be performed in outpatient labs adjacent to or in hospitals, but should not be performed in free-standing surgical or diagnostic centers away from the hospitals, according to recommendations from the American College of Physicians (ACP). The ACP guidelines suggest that outpatient cath labs perform the procedure only if they have immediate access to cardiac surgery in case of emergencies, and only if they are designed so that patients can be observed for four to six hours after having the cardiac cath. Also, the procedure should not be performed in outpatient labs on high-risk patients. The ideal patient for outpatient cardiac cath is an adult with stable coronary symptoms. Outpatient catheterization is contraindicated in the following cases:

- active congestive heart failure
- significant arrhythmias
- significant complicating conditions.

Patients who have complications during the cardiac cath or whose examinations indicate significant disease should be hospitalized immediately after the procedure.

Two Methods for the Cardiac Cath

There are basically two methods for performing cardiac caths, using the right femoral artery (the groin area of the right leg) and using the right brachial artery (the anterior area of the right elbow). When the femoral artery approach is used, patients should be kept in the recovery area for four hours in bed and two to four hours with limited movement before discharge. With the brachial artery approach, patients can have a much shorter recovery room time (two to four hours), and can be allowed up but with limited arm motion. Since the outpatient cath lab is normally operated only from 8 A.M. to 5 P.M., Monday through Friday, those patients having the femoral artery approach have to be catheterized very early in the day. Therefore, in order to maximize the efficiency of the cath lab and to minimize staffing costs, your cardiologists need to do the majority of the outpatient cardiac caths using the brachial artery approach.

Partners and Location

In developing a joint venture outpatient cath lab, the key to success lies in selecting those cardiologists who are looking ahead toward providing price-competitive services in an efficient outpatient setting. Protection of current market share is one of the strong motivators for aggressively developing an outpatient cath lab.

The Organizational Model

A good way to organize the joint venture is with a limited partnership. This organizational model enables the physicians as limited partners to limit their liabilities and losses to only the amount they invest in the joint venture. As limited partners, the physicians cannot actively be involved in the management of the cath lab and can act only as passive investors. Those physicians who want to organize the venture as a general partnership can take an active role in management and operations, but also have to assume unlimited liability for any losses of the cath lab. Organizing the physicians into a subchapter S corporation in order to become co-general partners with the hospital permits the physicians to both limit liability and engage actively in decision making. Either way, the partnership model offers the benefits of sheltering income through depreciation and investment tax credit and provides good cash flow to the investors.

Location, Location, Location . . .

Since the ideal location for an outpatient cath lab is one with immediate access to a hospital, an adjacent medical office building is the best bet. The medical office building should be connected to the hospital by a tunnel or covered walkway and should have the same floor access or stretcher size elevators. An outpatient cath lab requires approximately 2,400 gross square feet of space to accommodate a high volume of patients. If an outpatient surgery center is located in the same building or very close to it, the cath lab can be built adjacent to the surgery center. This can reduce the space requirements by 30 to 40 percent. An outpatient surgery center and cath lab can jointly share the registration and office functions, waiting room, and recovery room areas. Built as part of an outpatient surgery center, the cath lab can occupy as little as 1,400 square feet and purchase services and personnel from the surgery center on a very cost-effective basis. Either way, the outpatient cath lab offers a more convenient, cost-effective service than those based within inpatient facilities. With the increasing emphasis on ambulatory services that reduce inpatient costs, the outpatient cath lab may be the right joint venture for your hospital and your cardiologists.

Fighting the Competition

Even if cardiac catheterization procedures represent an increasing service in your hospital, you must realize that if you don't build an outpatient cath lab, someone else may—especially your competitors. If another party does offer to build your cardiologists their own outpatient cath lab, you may find yourself in the politically uncomfortable position of having to fight against your own physicians, especially in a public Certificate of Need (CON) forum. This becomes particularly awkward when your competitor's outpatient cath lab can usually demonstrate a safer, lower cost, and more convenient service—which just happens to involve your cardiologists. Similar situations arose for many hospitals with outpatient surgery centers. If you take the initiative now, you may well head off these problems by providing your cardiologists with a good investment opportunity that they understand and can significantly influence. At the same time, you will be protecting your market share by offering a safe, convenient, and cost-effective service.

What Does a Cath Lab Cost?

Once you have set up your investment objectives between the investors and decided upon the partnership model that fits your local situation, you are ready to develop a pro forma cash-flow projection and your business and marketing plan.

Regardless of how the joint venture is structured, a certain level of patient revenues and annual costs need to be established. An annual pro forma cash-flow statement for a volume of 1,000 cardiac cath lab procedures at $900 per procedure is shown in Exhibit 3-2.

This example is based on a 1,400-square-foot cath lab built adjacent to an outpatient surgery center and purchasing services and staff for registration, waiting room, and the recovery room. Those not built adjacent to surgery centers will have to increase their total operating costs by approximately 10 percent. Also, those cath labs that are built on the basis of a lower patient volume (500 to 800 per year) will realize fewer economies of scale and efficiencies. If the depreciation and investment tax credit benefits are also taken into consideration at the 50 percent tax bracket, the cath lab has an annual first-year total economic benefit of $300,000 to be distributed to the investors. Since most hospital-based cath labs charge between $1,000 and $1,200 per procedure, the outpatient joint venture can be extremely price competitive but can still discount heavily to protect market share if competition dictates. This could be especially important if the cardiac cath procedures are packaged together with open-heart surgery to form an all-inclusive total price for an HMO or PPO bid. Also, the hospital's inpatient facilities can be freed up for higher risk patients and the more complicated angioplasty and angiography procedures.

In many highly competitive markets, it may be necessary to move quickly before cardiac caths become price sensitive and follow the same path as outpatient surgery centers. Hospitals in these markets need to be prepared to have as many as 60 percent of their cardiac caths moved to an

---

Exhibit 3-2 Pro Forma for Cardiac Cath Lab

Patient revenue	$900,000	(1,000 × $900)
Less deductions	$45,000	(5% for bad debts)
Net operating revenue	$855,000	
Direct operating expenses		
Total payroll	$75,000	(3 FTEs)
Chargeable supplies	$225,000	($225/case)
Other medical supplies	$70,000	($70/case)
Purchased services	$80,000	($80/case)
Management fees	$45,000	(5% of gross revenues)
Other	$30,000	($30/case)
Total direct	$525,000	
Indirect expense		
Fixed lease	$16,000	($11.25/sq. ft. × 1,400 sq. ft.)
Utilities and cleaning	$9,000	($6.75/sq. ft. × 1,400 sq. ft.)
Long-term debt service	$109,000	($671,500@10% × 10 yrs.)
Short-term interest—working capital	$13,000	($90,000@14% × 1 yr.)
Total indirect	$147,000	
Net cash flow	$183,000	
Charge per case	$900	
Cost per case	$672	

outpatient setting. A joint venture between the hospital and the cardiologists offers a good opportunity to ensure that the outpatient cardiac caths stay within the overall system rather than going to a competitor. A partnership venture gets the physician economically invested with the hospital for several years and provides a framework for other joint ventures in the future.

Other Benefits for the Hospital

In a DRG or prospective priced system, an outpatient cath lab can further reduce the length of stay and provide increased financial margins. Since many professional review organizations (PROs) are restricting the payment for those DRGs where both cardiac cath and open-heart surgery are performed in the same episode, the outpatient cath lab maximizes payments for those DRGs and further reduces the chances that the cardiac surgery payment will be disallowed or reduced.

Before an outpatient lab is built, the objectives of the joint venture need to be firmly established. Is it to retain market share and be extremely price competitive, or is it primarily to provide a return on investment for the physicians? The more invasive cardiologists involved in the joint venture, the more likely will be the chance of success. Pricing strategies, equipment selection, and staffing levels all need to be agreed upon in advance and included in the business and marketing plan. Additionally, provisions for noninvestor cardiologists to use the new lab need to be defined, as well as provisions for adding additional physician investors in the future.

Cardiac catheterization can be performed safety as an outpatient procedure, reducing the cost to the patient of time and money (20 to 30 percent) and helping to alleviate demands for hospital inpatient space and staff.

Hospitals must face the facts by realizing that their hospital-based outpatient services are extremely vulnerable to outside joint ventures. Remembering the old adage, "a percentage of something is better than all of nothing," will help guide hospitals as they develop economic joint ventures with their physicians for outpatient services. Those that take the initiative and joint venture an outpatient cath lab between the hospital and interested cardiologists can protect or increase market share and achieve a competitive advantage.

THE MeSH: A UNIQUE PHYSICIAN INCENTIVE PLAN

What Is a MeSH?

A MeSH is a particular type of joint venture between hospitals and physicians. It can be described as a structural marriage between the hospital and its own medical staff. As noted earlier, it means *Me*dical *S*taff *H*ospital.

Who Developed the MeSH concept?

The concept was developed by InterStudy, a Minnesota health policy research organization.

Why Marry into a MeSH?

Why indeed? By forming a MeSH, the hospital and its medical staff are preparing themselves for a future in which they have a structure to deal with changes and opportunities in the health care marketplace.

What Does a MeSH Do?

It provides physicians and hospitals with the right organizational form to deal with the changing health care environment with its increased competition, increased costs, pressure to reduce charges, and other forces.

How Does a MeSH Work?

The core of the MeSH represents the common interests of both physicians and hospitals, providing for such services as management, planning, and marketing. It also provides for the formation of MeSH plans, a type of subcorporation designed to relate more directly to individual payers. Only physicians or hospitals that provide services to a particular payer group such as a particular HMO, for example, participate in the specific MeSH plan or subcorporation.

What Form Does the MeSH Take?

The form of the MeSH can be contractual, it can be a partnership, it can be a corporation, but the corporate structure usually is the most appropriate because it offers limited liability, relative ease of management, relative ease of governance, assignment of managerial responsibilities, and an understood framework that allows a large number of physicians to select leadership that can participate in governance.

What Are the Advantages of the MeSH

1. It creates a harmonious relationship between the hospital and its medical staff.

2. It creates a decision-making body that can help resolve hospital staff problems on a continuing basis.
3. It creates the ability to develop valid and valuable outreach entities.

Advantages of a MeSH

1. A MeSH has the flexibility to meet the needs of hospitals and physicians in achieving prospective payment targets.
2. Many of the new payment arrangements measure the cost of care as a combination of physician-generated services and hospital services. A MeSH can coordinate the delivery and management of physician and hospital care through joint decision making and involvement.
3. A MeSH offers physicians the opportunity to determine which competitive provider arrangements they desire to participate in.
4. Physicians and hospitals share the risk for revenues in a MeSH. This unique operational relationship can enhance productivity, utilization, and cost efficiency.

What Is the Downside of a MeSH?

While both sides—hospital and physicians—share in development and operating costs and have an equal number of representatives on the MeSH board, both sides give up some overall control. It also is a clumsy decision-making process that needs aggressive management techniques to create committees.

HOSPITALS AND LONG-TERM CARE FACILITIES

> Joint arrangements between hospitals and long-term care facilities pose possibilities for investment and enhancement of market position.*

The Hospital's Point of View

1. Access to long-term care beds can be helpful in responding to the incentives of PPS.

---

*Adapted from *Health Law Outlook,* Vol. 5, No. 1, with permission of Wood, Lucksinger & Epstein, Houston, © January 1986.

2. PPS has resulted in the decline overall of the average length of hospital stay and overall occupancy nationwide.
3. Hospitals may feel pressure from Medicare to receive some economic return from vacant space.
4. Few hospitals alone have the experience to provide the psychosocial aspects of long-term care cost effectively.

The Long-Term Care Facility's Point of View

1. The joint venture could provide a source of patients.
2. Conversion may be less costly than construction of a new facility.
3. Joint ownership provides for additional sources of capital and the sharing of risks.
4. Affiliation with a reputable hospital can enhance credibility.

WHAT TO WATCH OUT FOR: SIGNALS THAT MIGHT SPELL DANGER

- On the federal level, there may be serious risk that a not-for-profit hospital might lose its tax-exempt status if it forms a business alliance or coventure with a for-profit company.
- On the state level, the same danger might exist and jeopardize the not-for-profit's property tax exemption.
- The execution of a management contract under such coventures may raise issues of reimbursement from public payers that could affect the pricing of the contract and the degree of control retained by the facility hiring the management company.
- There may be federal tax implications where a tax-exempt entity hires a for-profit entity to manage any part of its operation. As a general rule, these contracts should be at arm's length, the exempt entity should maintain control of the business functions, it should not pay more than the fair market value for the management services, and the payment contract should not be based on the net revenues received from operations.
- Medicare and Medicaid antifraud and abuse provisions prohibit the knowing and willful soliciting, receiving, offering, or paying of any remuneration in return for the referral of patients or customers or the

generation of business for the party furnishing the remuneration. These provisions call for criminal penalties of up to five years' imprisonment and/or $25,000 in fines for each violation.

HOSPITALS AND HOME HEALTH CARE VENTURES

By 1988 about 30,000 patients will be receiving home nutrition therapy—the core business of the home infusion market. This market has a 20-to-30 percent pretax profit margin. Only about 75 to 100 of the larger teaching hospitals nationwide are suited for entry into the business through a joint venture with a home health care provider.

TEACHING HOSPITALS AND FOR-PROFITS

A recent study by A.T. Kearney, Inc., of Chicago of joint ventures involving teaching hospitals and for-profit hospitals reports:

- Joint ventures between teaching hospitals and for-profits developed mainly after 1984.
- Most of the agreements or joint ventures involved teaching hospitals and the top four for-profit chains: Hospital Corp. of America, Nashville; Humana Inc., Louisville; American Medical International, Beverly Hills, Cal.; and National Medical Enterprises, Los Angeles.
- Agreements give both parties something to shoot for: teaching hospitals satisfy their need for capital and a sustained patient base while the for-profits strengthen their presence in target markets.
- The cost of acquiring teaching hospitals has ranged from $188,000 to more than $332,000 per bed.
- For-profit chains in nearly all cases are willing to include a buyback future sale option if that is desired by the teaching hospital being purchased.

HOSPITALS WITH OTHER ENTITIES

In addition to some of the more traditional arrangements, hospitals also are forming joint ventures with insurance companies, HMOs, and health care organizations.

There is no lack out there in today's health care market of partners for joint ventures. Suddenly, hospitals have become attractive to business partners and are seen as strong moneymakers. Hospitals also are finding new life and vigor in joint ventures with all manner of business partners.

WRAP-UP

It is to be noted that the joint venture partner is often as significant a success or failure factor as joint venture product itself. Before embarking on a partnership remember, as in a marriage, you may have to spend a long time in bed together, so choose your partners carefully.

RED FLAGS

- Don't be a copycat joint-venture partner. Choose the appropriate partner and beware of pressure.
- Don't expect too much from your partner. Be realistic. But if it isn't working, get a divorce.
- Beware of ventures that are too innovative. If you've never done one before, go with the ones that have worked for other hospitals.
- Beware of mixing corporate cultures or corporate ethics. You can't expect your partners to compromise theirs, nor should you compromise yours.
- Don't do too many joint ventures at one time. Do a few strong ones and don't waste time on the weak ones.

CHECKLIST

Laundry List of Prospective Partners
Check which fit you best:

1. Physician groups and hospitals
2. Individual physicians and hospitals
3. Hospitals and long-term facilities
4. Hospitals and home health service companies
5. Teaching hospitals with for-profits
6. Hospitals and private for-profit industry
7. Hospitals and insurance companies

8. Hospitals and HMOs
9. HMOs, insurance companies, and multis

Put in order of importance your objectives for joint venturing:

1. New source of capital
2. Increase in revenue base
3. Economies of scale
4. Update in technology
5. Maintenance of current business
6. Reduction of costs
7. Sharing of financial risks and rewards
8. Introduction of new patient markets
9. Increase in physician alliances
10. Improvement in productivity
11. Provision of management expertise
12. Increase in employer/employee commitment

Checklist of possible ventures with 'Docs'

- Ambulatory care centers
- Surgery centers
- Urgent care centers
- Magnetic imaging diagnostic centers
- Other diagnostic facilities
- HMOs
- PPOs
- Medical office buildings
- Laundry facilities
- Long-term care programs

Chapter 4

Financing the Joint Venture*

Joan M. Annett

> FINANCE IS THE ART OF PASSING MONEY FROM ONE HAND TO ANOTHER UNTIL IT FINALLY DISAPPEARS.
>
> *Leonard L. Levinson*

*Adapted from "Financing Joint Ventures: The Planning and Selection Process" by Joan M. Annett in *Topics in Health Care Financing,* Vol. 12, No. 2, pp. 11–23, Aspen Publishers, Inc., © 1985.

HIGHLIGHTS

- The Imperfect Market Meets the Perfect Investment
- The Planning and Selection Process
- Screening Criteria for Financial Options
- Sources of Equity
- Sources of Debt Financing
- The Urgent Care Example
- Secured Debt
- Public vs. Private Offerings
- Enter the Venture Capitalist
- Partnerships
- Self-Financing: The Biggie
- Establishing values for screening criteria
- Exploring financing options

4

OPTIMUM FINANCIAL STRATEGIES

You have found an exciting business opportunity. You have done your market assessment. You are convinced that there is a need for your product and that, with the right marketing approach, there will be strong demand. Your feasibility analysis tells you there is money to be made, and your financial projections tell you how much capital you will need to get started.

You turn to your financial adviser to determine how to secure financing. You then experience the frustration of being presented with a seemingly infinite array of financing combinations to explore.

> You ask: "What is the optimum financial strategy for *this* venture?" The reply no doubt will be: "It depends."

When You've Seen One Venture—You've Seen One Venture

The problem has been nicely summarized by a leading attorney in the field of joint venture development.

> When you've seen one joint venture, you've seen one joint venture.

Hospital administrators will save weeks, even months, of frustration by accepting this maxim at the start of the process of selecting a financing option: There is no one "best" way to finance a joint venture. The number of institutional or individual sources of funds, multiplied by the mix of terms acceptable to each source, multiplied by the combination of sources possibly needed to complete the financing package, creates too many options to analyze.

The Imperfect Market Meets the Perfect Investment

The sources of joint-venture financing exist in what may be termed an imperfect market. On one side are many individuals or institutional sources of funds looking for investment or loan opportunities, and on the other side many ventures searching for funds. However, there is no central market or clearing house (such as the New York Stock Exchange) to bring these buyers and sellers together. In addition, the players in this market—both buyers and sellers—are changing constantly.

> Hence, the hospital administrator who focuses on getting the "best" financing deal is aiming for the proverbial moving target.

None of this is meant to discourage the process of searching for better alternatives. It is to suggest that the strategy should focus on finding acceptable alternatives, rather than optimum alternatives, to avoid unnecessary delay. There is a method for searching systematically through a reasonable variety of options. It involves weighing the advantages and disadvantages of each option in relation to criteria that have been determined necessary to qualify an acceptable candidate for final selection.

A Caveat

Figure 4-1 illustrates the overall joint-venture planning process to set the context in which the financing, planning, and selection process (Figure 4-2) takes place. A sense of lack of direction in choosing among options often comes from failing to understand that a financing plan is a means to achieve an overall business strategy, not an end in itself.

It is not uncommon for the business planner to move comfortably and confidently through the goal-setting, market assessment, and feasibility stages of a plan. However, on arriving at the financing stage and being given a laundry list of choices, each with important market and financial implications, that same planner wants to redefine the underlying business

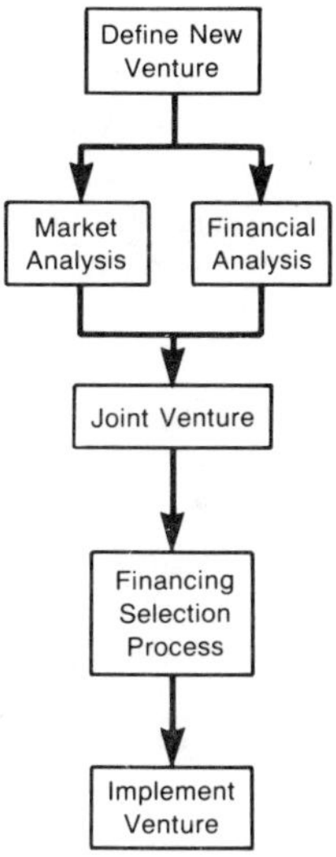

Figure 4-1 Overall Joint Venture Planning Process

plan in order to take advantage of particularly clever financing schemes. This leads to significant delays and confusion of purpose as the strategic planning process in effect starts all over again.

The knowledge gained and decisions made in the initial planning process (Figure 4-1) should feed directly into development of screening criteria. These criteria will define the variables in the financing, planning, and selection process (Figure 4-2) and thus maintain forward momentum and continuity between strategic and financing planning.

DEVELOPING SCREENING CRITERIA

The decision to pursue a joint venture is a product of one or a combination of three situations.

SITUATION 1

You lack certain technical, management, or marketing resources. You are seeking a joint-venture partner(s) to provide these resources. For example, you are a hospital that wants to construct a medical office building (MOB) on its campus. However, management lacks construction or office building management skills.

Therefore, it is looking for a contractor/developer, with prior MOB experience, as a joint-venture partner. Or you are a physician who wants to open an urgent care center. You want to attract a well-respected hospital in the area as a partner to gain the market recognition and advantage of using the hospital's name.

SITUATION 2

You want to guarantee market share or lock out the competition. To expand on the MOB example in Situation 1, the hospital may want to include physicians as partners in the venture, recognizing that many will be inclined to rent office space in a building they own. Or a major for-profit hospital company may try to find joint venture partners for the development of an alcohol rehabilitation center with a local community hospital to prevent the latter from developing its own center.

SITUATION 3

You do not have sufficient capital to finance the venture alone, or you prefer to share the risk. For example, the physician In Situation 1 may not have sufficient capital or credit to finance a startup urgent care center and is hoping to get the hospital to put up cash or guarantee debt in exchange for part ownership.

Table 4-1 lists the types of screening criteria that should be considered: sources of funds, number of investors, amount, costs, term, liquidity, and percentage of ownership or control. Table 4-1 also illustrates how the values attached to each criterion vary, depending on the situation being analyzed.

For example, the first screening criterion considers the various sources of funds and distinguishes the many institutional and individual providers or purveyors of capital: commercial banks, tax-exempt bonds, private placements through insurance companies, venture capital funds, pension funds, personal savings, retained earnings, and limited partnership syndications.

Because tax-exempt bonds are available only to Sec. 501(c)(3) nonprofit corporations (as defined in the Internal Revenue Code) or to projects qualifying for industrial development bonds, the value of the screening criterion can be set to favor tax-exempt financing, taxable financing, or both. Similarly, unsecured bank loans normally are available only to es-

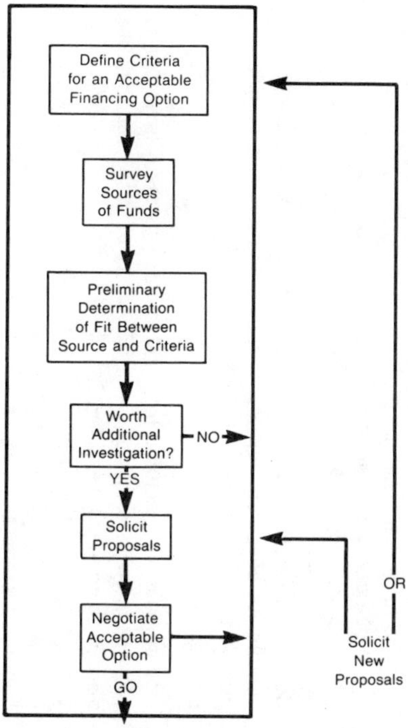

Figure 4-2 Joint Venture Financing, Planning, and Election Process

tablished businesses with at least three years of operating history. Thus, for startup ventures, the value of the screening criterion can be set to direct the planner to look at sources of funds that do not require a proved track record.

SURVEYING SOURCES OF CAPITAL

Once the screening criteria are defined, available sources of funds can be surveyed.

> **The classic distinction for sources of funds is between debt and equity sources of capital.**

In recent years, financing vehicles that combine debt and equity or that use credit enhancers have become increasingly popular ways to attract new sources of capital.

Table 4-1 Screening Criteria for Selecting Financing Options

	Value		
Type of screen	*Situation 1. Need technological, management, or marketing resources*	*Situation 2. Need to guarantee market or co-opt competitors*	*Situation 3. Need capital*
Source of funds, e.g., bank loan, tax-exempt bonds, venture capital, retained earnings	Source also must offer other needed resources, or not discourage desirable resource-providing partner(s).	Source also must offer competitive advantage, or not discourage market-enhancing partner.	Any source can be considered, subject to remaining criteria.
Number of investors	Option must be structured to allow as many investors as needed to obtain needed resources. Generally one or two is sufficient.	Option must be structured to allow as many investors as needed to enhance market position, e.g., may need to allow participation by several hundred members of hospital's medical staff.	Must allow as many investors as necessary to raise needed capital.
Amount	Size of investment opportunity must be sufficient to gain partner's commitment.	Size of investment opportunity must be sufficient to hold partner's loyalty and use.	Size of investment must be sufficient to raise needed capital.
Initial and annual costs	Not relevant as long as financial feasibility is not impaired (to be determined by measuring the sensitivity of the financial projections to different levels of financing costs).	Same as for Situation 1.	Need to determine relationship between venture's rate of return and financing costs. Cost of financing alternative should be equal to or less than that needed to obtain desired rate of return.

Term, i.e., length of time for which financing is made available	At a minimum, must meet cash-flow needs of venture but also should accommodate investment time needs of resource providers to attract them as investors.	At a minimum, must meet cash-flow needs of venture but also should seek to accommodate investment time needs of market-enhancers/competitors to attract them as investors.	Must meet cash-flow needs of venture.
Liquidity, i.e., ability to minimize losses of the venture or to use its assets for other purposes by quickly converting to cash.	Must accommodate liquidity preferences of venture's originator and other investors who also are resource providers. If risk tolerance of each group is different, may need to structure different liquidity options.	Must accommodate liquidity preferences of venture's originator and other investors who also are market enhancers/competitors. If risk tolerance of each group is different, may need to structure different liquidity options.	Must meet criteria of venture's originator to minimize risk.
Percentage of ownership or control	Must retain sufficient ownership/control to meet financial return targets but also give sufficient ownership/control to attract commitment of high-quality resource providers.	Must retain sufficient ownership/control to meet financial return and market control goals. Must also give enough ownership/control to partners to ensure their loyalty and use.	Need to retain only as much ownership/control as necessary to ensure success of venture and to meet financial return targets.

Debt

Table 4-2 summarizes the important characteristics and purveyors of debt financing. It also distinguishes between tax-exempt and taxable instruments.

Much attention has been focused on the ability of hospitals and other 501(c)(3) nonprofit health care organizations to borrow at tax-exempt rates ranging from 50 to 60 percent of the prime rate for short-term debt (seven days to three years) and 85 to 95 percent of prime for long-term debt (20 to 30 years). Access to this relatively inexpensive source of debt capital is a major asset that any 501(c)(3) nonprofit organization brings to a joint venture, although care must be taken to preserve tax-exempt status in structuring the financing if the venture involves for-profit partners (such as physicians) or nonexempt purposes (such as a parking garage or an MOB).

The Urgent Care Example

For example, if a hospital and its medical staff want to cooperate in the development of a free-standing urgent care center using proceeds from tax-exempt bonds issued by the hospital, the physicians' role may have to be structured as a management contract for staffing and operating the facility.

In general, rules against use of tax-exempt debt for nonexempt purposes can be avoided if the nonexempt uses are only a small proportion (generally less than 20 percent) of the total tax-exempt debt being issued.

'Blind' Pools

A sophisticated yet simple use of tax-exempt debt by hospitals in financing joint ventures is through the issuance of "blind" equipment-financing pools. These instruments, which normally are issued as short- or medium-term debt, allow the creation of a pool of capital to be used over three years for tax-exempt purposes unspecified at the time of issuance of the bonds (hence a blind pool). Purchases such as routine capital additions, which in the past would have been paid out of retained earnings, can be paid from the blind pool account. This frees up retained earnings to be used for investing in for-profit ventures with for-profit partners (subject to some additional but considerably less onerous qualifiers).

Industrial Development Bonds

One additional source of tax-exempt funds for joint ventures is small issue industrial development bonds (IDBs). These are debt securities issued by a government entity on behalf of an otherwise nonexempt party. Basically, an issue qualifies as a small issue IDB if it is for $10 million or less, or if the amount of the issue, together with the issuing entity's total capital expenditures for the three years preceding and three years following the issue date, is not in excess of $10 million. The $10 million limit does not present an insurmountable obstacle for many health care joint venture opportunities, although additional restrictions can be imposed by local governments. There also are bills pending in Congress to further curtail the use of this financing mechanism.

As Table 4-2 indicates, taxable debt options range from private placements with insurance companies or pension funds, to bank loans, to publicly offered bonds. Historically, interest rates for taxable issues have been 2 to 3 percent higher than these for comparable tax-exempt financing, although in recent years the spread between these two forms of debt has narrowed. Most lenders require a minimum three-year profit history and a stable environment before making an unsecured loan. Even in those circumstances, they often will require asset pledges or personal guarantees of the debt.

The Risk of Joint Ventures

Given the high degree of business risk associated with many health care joint ventures, secured debt often is the only option available.

TYPES OF SECURED DEBT

- The most common forms of secured debt are mortgages, leases, and accounts receivable financing.
- Mortgages and leases are readily available for building or equipment acquisition because the acquired asset may be used to secure the debt instrument. These are popular sources of capital for startup ventures that are not otherwise able to attract capital.
- A sale-leaseback involves the sale of a facility or equipment to a lessor who then leases the facility back to the user. In essence, a sale-leaseback allows the user 100 percent financing for an asset.

Table 4-2 Sources of Taxable and Tax-Exempt Debt

Source	Term	*Characteristics* *Security Provisions*	*Costs*
Tax-Exempt			
Short term: • variable rate demand notes (VRDNs) • commercial paper • bond anticipation notes (BANs)	7 days to 6 months for VRDNs and commercial paper; 1 to 3 years for BANs	Generally backed by bank letter of credit or line of credit. Usually available only to health care companies with at least an A-rating	Fixed or variable rate at 50–60% of prime; underwriter's discount: 1–2%, letter of credit fee 0.5–0.75% (+ annual letter of credit fee)
Long-term bonds	20 to 30 years, may be called or prepaid after 10 years	Gross revenue pledge, mortgage or negative pledge of assets can be insured by government or private programs	Insurance fees: 0.5–1%; interest rates 85–95% of prime; discount: 2.5 to 3.5%
Industrial development bonds (IDBs)	Can be either short-term or long-term (see above)	Mortgage revenue bonds, negative pledge, or gross revenues pledge	Costs tend to range at upper end of scale because of the small size and complexity
Blind pools: • multiple facility • single entity	Can be either short term (VRDNs) or conventional long term	If needed, pool can be supported by letter or line of credit. Multiple facility pools also can require individual credit report or enhancer before releasing funds	Same as short-term or long-term bonds
Taxable			
Short term: • line of credit • letter of credit	Lines of credit typically 1 year; letters of credit can go up to 5 years	Generally need a strong credit rating and history. Lines are often unsecured. Revolving lines must be paid up once a year. Borrower covenants to maintain certain financial	Rate usually floats but can be fixed for 6-month to 2-year term. Annual fees of 0.5–1% on unused line. Letter of credit fees of 0.5–1.5% per year.

		personal guarantees or pledges of all unsecured assets	
Asset-based financing	Renewable	Pledge of accounts receivable	Prime + 2 to 4%
Mortgages	Often 5 to 15 years amortized over 25 years, with a balloon payment	Secured by real property	Commercial rates are 2–5% points up front and 13–15%. Rates are 2–5% lower if lender receives a percentage of gross profits
Leases	If a financing lease, same as useful life of asset. Operating leases range between month-to-month and 5+ years. Sale-lease-backs often involve 15- to 30-year lease terms	Secured by lease asset	10–25% down payment, 18%+ per year with nominal (financing lease) or market price buyout (operating lease) at end of the term; sale-leaseback rates are comparable to mortgages, or lower if tax benefits are available to lender
Long-term: • bonds • convertible debt • preferred stock	For bonds: up to 30 years. Conversion date for convertible debt can vary between 1 and 10 years. Indefinite for preferred stock	Publicly traded bonds are generally available only to established, financially strong companies. "Junk bonds" for less credit-worthy companies can be privately placed with specialty funds. Private placements sometimes available from pension funds and insurance companies. Convertible debt is a favorite venture capital vehicle. Preferred stock is usually purchased by corporations to gain tax-free income	As of 3/85, industrials rated AA were 12.5%. Junk bonds have traded up to 20%. Rate and value of convertible debt varies with risk of venture and price of conversion. Preferred stock returns are comparable to rates on bonds

EQUITY . . . EQUITY . . . AND EQUITY AGAIN

Pluses of Equity Financing

Equity financing offers many advantages over debt financing. Debt financings generally are tied to specific projects or assets. Equity proceeds usually are not restricted and therefore can be used to finance more general business activities, such as working capital or operations.

Equity proceeds also increase the debt capacity of a company, thus providing a base for raising even more capital.

Equity financing involves selling part of the ownership of an enterprise and thus can be an effective means of attracting desirable business associates and employees.

However, in this as in most everything, there also is a down side.

> The major disadvantages of equity financing are diminished control and, frequently, high transaction costs.

Categories of Equity Financing

Most equity financings fall into one of three categories:

1. stock offerings
2. partnerships
3. self-financing.

Stock Offerings

Stock offerings can be further subdivided into public offerings, private offerings, and issuing options and warrants. Table 4-3 summarizes the major types and sources of equity.

Public Stock Offerings: The Glamour and the Flash

Public stock offerings are the glamour area of capital finance.

> Unfortunately, the excitement surrounding initial public offerings in recent years has obscured the high cost of these issues.

Table 4-3 Sources of Equity

Type	*Source*
Stock Offerings	
Public stock offering	Stock is sold to the public at large. Investment bankers are needed to serve as underwriters and to market the shares.
Private stock offering	Stock is sold directly to large investors such as insurance companies, commercial banks, pension funds, or wealthy individuals. Does not require an underwriter, but often uses an investment banker to serve as broker.
Options and warrants	Commonly used for employee incentive plans. Increasingly used as partial compensation to suppliers. Are popular with venture capitalists because they increase the venture capitalist's ownership without requiring immediate cash payment.
Partnerships	
General	Generally privately placed. Best where all parties want active involvement in the operations of the business. Also appropriate where individuals wish to pass the business' gains and losses through to their personal income tax returns.
Limited	Can be privately placed or publicly syndicated. Most attractive to individuals who want substantial tax advantages, yet do not want the liability obligations or operations involvement of a general partner.
Self-Financing	
By owner	Personal savings, pledges of personal assets, family investment.
By employees	Employees are indirect sources of capital when they agree to incentive-based and deferred compensation rather than guaranteed salaries. Employee stock purchase and option plans are common vehicles.

The cost of a public issue of stock typically ranges from $250,000 to $500,000 for costs of issuance, 7–10 percent underwriter's discount, and the continuing costs and reporting requirements imposed by the Securities and Exchange Commission (SEC) on publicly owned corporations.

Private Stock Offerings: Enter the Venture Capitalist

Private stock offerings to small groups of investors, often through venture capital funds, are an increasingly commonplace form of capital financing. Venture capitalists invest in new businesses that have high profit potential but, because of lack of historical performance, may not have access to the debt or public equity markets.

> Venture capital firms supply new businesses with needed capital in return for a share of ownership that they usually hope to market to the public at a later date.

In 1982 and 1983 health care high-technology and alternative delivery startup ventures were popular among venture capitalists. However, because many of these stocks later were selling below their initial offering price, venture capital in the health care industry became more difficult to find. Overall, any fluctuations in share prices affect the availability of venture capital, so market conditions in general can have an impact. Sometimes it is prudent to delay a venture if the market and funding sources so indicate.

In relation to public stock offerings, the advantages of private venture capital issues are lower front-end issuance and transaction costs, negotiable structure and terms, reduced reporting requirements, and, perhaps most important, access to the experience and business acumen of the venture capital investors. The primary disadvantage of private issues versus public offerings is that private issues generally require transfer of a greater ownership share to obtain the same amount of financing.

Options and Warrants

Options and warrants are rights to buy stock at a certain price within a specified time period. Generally, no capital payment is required until the option or warrant is exercised.

> Options are popular devices for recruiting and retaining desirable employees.

They create a proprietary commitment to the company's success without requiring an immediate payment of cash. Warrants typically are granted in connection with the sale of stock. They make the stock more attractive by giving the buyer the right to acquire future shares at current prices.

Partnerships

Partnerships are alternative ways of organizing equity investments in joint ventures. A general partnership joint venture differs from a stockholder corporation in two important aspects.

> 1. In a stockholder corporation, investors' earnings are taxed twice—once when the corporation pays taxes on dividend income, once then the dividend receiver pays taxes on their income.
> 2. In a partnership, all earnings (or losses, including tax benefits) are passed along directly to the partners' tax returns so that they are taxed only once.

Although stockholders can lose the value of their investment in a joint venture, they cannot be held liable for any additional losses or claims against the corporation. General partners do not enjoy this protection. Each partner is considered personally liable for any and all of the partnership's obligations.

. . . Enter the Limited Partner

A popular variation in a general partnership is to allow for limited partners as investors. Limited partners enjoy the same type of limited liability as stockholders, yet still get direct pass-through of all earnings and tax benefits. The trade-off is that limited partners are prohibited from involvement in management of the venture. Limited partnerships are ideal tax-oriented investment vehicles for individuals who do not want the liability or operations involvement of a general partner.

Self-Financing—The Biggie

Self-financing undoubtedly remains the single largest source of equity capital for joint venture health care projects. The inherent risk and small size of these projects can result in the owners' being the only sources willing to back the venture.

> Self-financing also is popular because it guarantees management and governance control.

Incentive-related forms of self-financing, such as salary reductions in exchange for ownership shares, and classic entrepreneurial vehicles for financing high-risk start-up ventures.

The Equity-Debt Duo

Because the supply of capital for new ventures has lagged behind demand in recent years, new entries into the market increasingly have resorted to complex combinations of venture capital, debt, limited partnerships, and leases to attract new sources of capital. For example, banks, often reluctant to lend to startup ventures, are being enticed with debt/equity packages that combine a below-market rate on a loan with a percentage of gross revenues as the business grows.

Explosive Entrant in the $$$ Game

A potentially explosive factor in the capital financing market for health care joint ventures is the entry of the large proprietary hospital chains and drug and supply companies into funding joint ventures. For example, in response to medical staff demands and to competition from entrepreneurs, American Medical International has reversed its opposition to entering joint ventures with physicians.

> **Health care joint venture developers can take advantage of these changing corporate priorities by using strategies pioneered by high-technology startup ventures for attracting corporate investors.**

Good corporate investment partners include suppliers or distributors. For example, all of the major pharmaceutical companies are soliciting partnerships with home health care agencies to ensure future markets for their home therapy products. Other fertile sources are companies hoping for access to new technology or products. For example, a computer software company might agree to underwrite a health maintenance organization's (HMO's) cost of developing a budgeting system in return for rights to sell the package to other HMOs.

ESTABLISHING SCREENING CRITERIA VALUES

The following are examples of how the entrepreneur can establish values for the screening criteria:

- *Source:* Area hospitals obviously are a primary source of capital. Bank loans are a possibility as long as the terms are not unduly restrictive in permitting hospital partners to join. A tax-oriented financing vehicle is an ideal option because it allows the venture to transfer the investment tax credits and depreciation write-off benefits accruing to any of its nonprofit hospital partners in return for low-cost capital.
- *Number of Investors:* The entrepreneurs may decide to limit the number of hospital partners to 35 or fewer to avoid cumbersome SEC registration requirements.
- *Amount:* Entrepreneurs need to structure the partnerships to encourage the hospitals to make substantial equity commitments and to attract debt capital at a reasonable rate. (Lenders generally will finance startup ventures only if these are substantial investor contributions.)
- *Costs:* Entrepreneurs have done sensitivity analyses on their cash-flow projections and determined that they cannot support more than $100,000 in front-end financing costs and greater than 12 percent in annual interest costs.
- *Term:* Entrepreneurs need a five-year commitment of first-round capital.
- *Liquidity:* This is not, by nature, a liquid investment. Some attempt to structure liquidity, such as guaranteed buyout provisions at the end of year 3, would aid greatly in attracting hospital partners.
- *Percentage of Ownership or Control:* Entrepreneurs are willing to reduce their percentage ownership if, by bringing in partners, they can guarantee a larger business. They think it is important that control be vested in an authority independent from hospitals. They personally do not need to retain this role, particularily once the venture is running well.

EXPLORING THE FINANCING OPTIONS

Tax-Exempt Debt

Entrepreneurs can quickly rule out IDBs as a source, given their total capital needs of $12 million. They still can tap into tax-exempt funds by encouraging their potential hospital partners to finance their investment through blind equipment pools or as a defined part of a hospital-specific tax-exempt bond issue.

Taxable Debt

Many sources can be explored for additional debt financing. Leases secured by the equipment assets can provide funds. A technique popular among high-technology firms is to eliminate the down payment on any lease by getting suppliers to accept stock warrants or options. A commercial bank loan is a remote possibility because this is a startup venture. However, such a loan is possible if the hospital partners agree to guarantee the venture's debt.

Equity

The entrepreneurs already have indicated their intention to have their hospital partners supply most of the venture's capital. They also may consider using personal savings and starting an employee stock ownership plan.

> Another good candidate for low-cost equity is developing a tax-oriented limited partnership to purchase the durable medical equipment as a vehicle for transferring excess investment tax credits and depreciation benefits to for-profit entities.

Entrepreneurs should think about marketing these partnerships to physicians as a means of capturing their referrals in addition to hospital-based referrals.

WRAP-UP

Joint ventures offering real value will always find funding. Venture originators can be expected to look increasingly to unconventional sources of funds, such as distributors and suppliers, and to complex packages of debt and equity tailored to attract desired investors. Choosing among capital financing vehicles involves careful attention to goals such as establishing market strategies, gaining technology or management expertise, and co-opting competitors.

Given the number of variables involved, and their constantly changing nature, the goal should be to establish the acceptable parameters of a financing package, select one that falls within those limits, and get on with implementation.

RED FLAGS

- Be aware that the hunt for the perfect financial package can be long and hard. Don't take any shortcuts.
- Be aware that a lack of direction in choosing among financing options often comes from failing to understand that a financing plan is a means to achieve an overall business strategy, not an end in itself.
- Watch your tax-exempt status if it applies.
- Understand that this is a risky business and govern yourself and your hospital accordingly.
- Be very clear on what you are giving away when you arrange for financing for your joint venture. Where is the control—with you, or with the capital?

Chapter 5

Tax Aspects of Hospital-Physician Joint Ventures*

Douglas M. Mancino

THOSE WHO ARE PROSPERING DO NOT ARGUE ABOUT TAXES.

Ancient Chinese proverb

*Adapted from "Tax Aspects of Hospital-Physician Joint Ventures" by Douglas M. Mancino in *Topics in Health Care Financing*, Vol. 12, No. 2, pp. 46–51, Aspen Publishers, Inc., © 1985.

HIGHLIGHTS

- Effect of Changing Health Care Environment on Hospitals
- Tax Implications of Hospital-Physician Joint Ventures
- Contractual and partnership models
- The corporate model
- Comparison of tax advantages
- Joint ventures and nonprofit hospitals
- Planning opportunities and pitfalls
- General tax considerations

5

The hospital industry faces unprecedented competitive and financial demands. As the number of physicians, nursing homes, health maintenance organizations, hospitals, and free-standing ambulatory care clinics has grown, competition between and among health care providers has increased. In addition, various organizations predict an unprecedented demand for capital investment to renovate, replace, expand, and modernize hospitals and health care facilities. At the same time, the ever-present impact of federal and state regulation on health care organizations continues to be felt strongly.

> The changing health care environment has had many effects on hospitals. One of them has been to challenge traditional notions of medical staff-hospital relationships and to foster the growth of hospital-physician joint ventures.

TAX IMPLICATIONS

The tax implications of hospital-physician joint ventures depend on numerous variables, including the tax-exempt status of the hospital, the proposed business of the joint venture, the form of entity selected to conduct the joint venture, and the amount of leverage used to finance it.

Operating an MRI Center

For example, the tax aspects of a joint venture designed to operate a magnetic resonance imaging center (MRI) or an ambulatory surgery center differ markedly from those of a joint venture designed to construct and lease a professional office building. Moreover, when one of the participants in a joint venture is a tax-exempt hospital, or a for-profit or nonprofit affiliate of a tax-exempt hospital, special care is required to ensure that the tax-exempt status of the hospital, or its affiliates, is not affected adversely and that the joint venture is structured so as to minimize or eliminate any unrelated business taxable income.

The Joint Venture Form

One of the first decisions confronting hospitals and physicians desiring to pool their capital or services in a joint venture is the selection of the most appropriate form of business organization.

> There are many business and legal reasons why one form of joint venture may be selected over another, but it is seldom that the choice between corporate and partnership forms is compelled by nontax considerations.

The Contractual Models

The contractual form of joint venture is probably the simplest type of structure from a tax standpoint. The hospital entering into the contract with the physician, to the extent it retains the ownership of the equipment or facilities used in the joint venture, also is entitled to enjoy the tax benefits available to owners of capital assets. The physicians, being lessees or mere users of the equipment or facilities, generally are not entitled to the tax benefits of capital asset ownership, with certain limited exceptions.

The Partnership Model

A partnership is not subject to federal or state income tax. Instead, the partners are taxed directly on partnership income, whether or not it actually is distributed to them. Similarly, partnership tax losses are passed to the partners and generally are deductible against taxable income derived from other sources.

In the case of partnership income, the effective rate of tax becomes a function of the tax brackets of the partners, which range from 11 to 50 percent of taxable income for individual partners, and 15 to 46 percent for corporate partners. For taxable years beginning in 1984, an extra 5 percent tax was added to the taxable income of a corporation in excess of $1 million until the graduated tax benefits on the first $100,000 of taxable income in effect had been eliminated.

The Corporate Model

Unlike partnerships, corporations are separate taxpaying entities. Income and losses derived by the corporation are taxable to or deductible by it and cannot be passed to its shareholders unless it qualifies for treatment as a Subchapter S corporation. If the corporation is eligible for, and elects treatment as an S corporation, income and loss generally will be taxable to or deductible by its shareholders and the corporation will not be taxed separately. The tax rates on corporate income range from 15 percent of the first $25,000 of taxable income to 46 percent on taxable income in excess of $100,000.

Although shareholders are not taxed on corporate income, they are taxable on its distributions. For example, to the extent a corporation declares dividends out of its current or accumulated earnings and profits, those distributions generally will be taxable to its shareholders at ordinary income tax rates.

> In many instances, a corporation may be a costly tax substitute for a partnership because maximum tax efficiency seldom can be achieved. Income earned through a corporate entity usually is subject to a double tax. The corporation will pay a tax on the immediate realization of income and the shareholder ultimately will pay a second tax on the distribution of such income.

The combined effective rate of double taxation will be a function of the rate of tax paid by the corporation, the marginal tax brackets of its shareholders, and the character of the income realized at the corporate and shareholder levels, either as a capital gain or as ordinary income.

COMPARISON OF TAX ADVANTAGES

The determination of which entity should be used from a tax standpoint will depend on a number of factors:

- If the joint venture is expected to generate substantial tax losses in its early years, a determination should be made as to whether those losses are better used as deductions against the venture's owners other income on a current basis or deferred for use as deductions against the future income of the joint venture itself. If the deductions are best used in the early years, then the partnership form should be selected, or an S corporation election should be made, if available. If the losses will be used more profitably to offset other income generated by the joint venture itself, then the corporate form may be the preferred structure and no S corporate election should be made.
- If a joint venture is expected to generate substantial taxable income, the participants must determine whether the income will be reinvested in the venture or distributed to its owners. If the income is to be reinvested, then the corporate form may be preferred to the partnership. If the joint venture does not require substantial investment of capital from operations, then the partnership form may be the preferred joint venture entity. Finally, because one or more corporate owners is likely to be involved (such as the hospital or one of its affiliates) the impact of double taxation is reduced substantially, if not eliminated, for the corporate owners.

JOINT VENTURES AND NONPROFIT HOSPITALS

Nonprofit hospitals enjoy exemption from federal income taxation under Section 501(a) of the Internal Revenue Code, typically because they qualify as charitable organizations described in Section 501(c)(3) of the Code. Section 501(c)(3) describes those entities.

> Organized and operated exclusively for . . . charitable, scientific, . . . or educational purpose. . . .

PRIVATE BENEFIT AND INUREMENT

In determining whether a nonprofit hospital, acting alone or in concert with other individuals or organizations, is furthering charitable purpose, the courts and the IRS consider whether its primary purpose is a charitable one, whether the means it employs are reasonably designed to accomplish the charitable purposes, and whether the scope of the charitable activity is commensurate with its resources. If a hospital engages in unrelated trade or business, its tax-exempt status will not be in jeopardy solely by reason of that trade or business.

> To maintain tax exempt status under Section 501(c)(3), no part of a hospital's net earnings may inure, in whole or in part, to the benefit of any private shareholder or individual.

The hospital also must be organized and operated to further a public purpose so it may not be designed for the benefit of private interests such as designated individuals or persons directly or indirectly controlling the charitable hospital.

When nonprofit hospitals become involved in joint ventures, the key concerns are twofold.

> 1. Whether any of the financial or nonfinancial arrangements contemplated by the joint venture results in the inurement of any portion of the nonprofit hospital's net earnings to the benefit of any private shareholder or individual.
> 2. Whether the participation in the joint venture, regardless of its form, confers a benefit on private interests that are so substantial as to provide evidence that the nonprofit hospital is operating for private benefit rather than for public purpose.

The prohibition against inurement of net earnings is directed toward the conferral of financial or similar benefits of insiders or other persons in control of a charitable organization, other than as reasonable compensation for service actually provided. This prohibition is likely to be of concern where the proposed joint venture involves the use or distribution of a hospital's assets through loans, leases, and compensation arrangements.

The private benefit challenge is likely to be raised when the business relationship is with persons more closely linked to the charitable hospital, such as members of the medical staff, even though they are not "private shareholders or individuals" within the meaning of the inurement prohibition.

In advancing the interests of a charitable hospital, in a case where private benefit may present a problem, it is incumbent on the parties to provide as much definitive evidence as possible of the benefits accruing to the institution from the joint venture and to establish some nexus between the benefits provided to the participants and the accomplishment of the facility's charitable purposes.

PLANNING OPPORTUNITIES AND PITFALLS

In the joint-venture context, potential challenges to tax-exempt status may arise in a number of situations. A discussion of some of the opportunities and pitfalls follows:

- Medical office buildings frequently are constructed by, or sold to, limited partnerships that include physician-tenants as limited partners.
- Exemption concerns are likely to arise if the building is to be constructed on land leased by the hospital or an affiliate to the limited partnership, or if the existing building is sold subject to a ground lease.
- Exemption problems can arise if the ground lease rents are fixed at a rate less than fair rental value. Similarly, it is quite common for lenders to request some form of credit enhancement from the hospital for the partnership's obligation. Providing a guarantee or other form of credit enhancement, apart from giving rise to other potential tax problems, can be viewed by the IRS as using assets for the benefit of private interest, particularly where no guarantee fee or other form of compensation is provided.
- Hospitals may be requested to make loans directly to the medical office building partnership. The IRS can be expected to scrutinize such loans to determine whether a market rate of interest is being charged and whether the repayment of the loan has been adequately secured by the assets of the partnership.
- The IRS, if interest rates are below market, or if the security is inadequate, may allege that the hospital is permitting a portion of its net earnings to go the benefit of private individuals or that such a transaction is evidence that the institution is serving private, rather than public, purposes.
- Care must be taken, when a joint venture is formed to operate a particular business, such as an ambulatory surgery center or a diagnostic imaging center, in structuring the division of profits and losses between the exempt and nonexempt participants.

- The IRS reviews carefully the manner used to divide profits, and generally expects that they will be split proportionate to the amount of capital invested.
- The hospital should be prepared to demonstrate, if there is a disproportionate allocation of profits and losses, or if there are attempts to specially allocate items of income, gain, loss, tax credits, and the like, that it is being compensated in a manner that provides for a fair return on its investment.

An exempt hospital can take many steps to minimize the jeopardy to its tax-exempt status.

- The terms and conditions of the joint venture should be comparable with those that would have been established had the arrangement been negotiated at arm's length. For example, the economic components of the transaction should be no less favorable to the hospital than would be the case if the transaction involved persons other than members of the medical staff.
- The joint venture should be structured to provide for buyouts and similar types of safeguards for the hospital's interests.
- Consideration should be given to obtaining an advance ruling from the IRS before proceeding with the joint venture. If time permits, this will provide assurances to the hospital that its tax-exempt status will not be jeopardized.

GENERAL TAX CONSIDERATIONS

Accelerated Cost Recovery System

The general rules for the accelerated cost recovery system (ACRS) are set forth in Section 168 of the Internal Revenue Code. The costs of personal property, such as medical equipment, can be recovered over a three- or five-year period, generally using rates that approximate the use of the 150 percent declining balance method during the early years, with conversion to the straight-line method in later years.

Similarly, the costs of real property may be recovered over an 18-year period. ACRS provides for an accelerated method of recovering costs, although the elective straight-line method can be chosen.

Investment Tax Credit

In addition to ACRS deductions, the joint venture may be eligible for an investment tax credit on any personal property purchased by it, including elevators and escalators. In general, a 10 percent credit will be allowed for investments in medical equipment that qualify as five-year recovery property. However, if the medical equipment qualifies as three-year recovery property, only a 6 percent credit will be allowed.

Tax-Exempt Use Property Rules

The Tax Reform Act of 1984 added a comprehensive set of rules to the Internal Revenue Code. It is designed to reduce or eliminate the tax benefits associated with property leased to, or otherwise used by, tax-exempt organizations. In general, the new changes deal with three basic areas.

1. New Section 168(j) provides that the recovery periods for real and personal property classified as tax-exempt use property will be greater than those for all other real or personal property.
2. New Section 7701(e) codifies the criteria to be used to distinguish service and other contracts from leases of real or personal property to tax exempt organizations.
3. Section 168(j) also contains several rules that are applicable to partnerships that have tax-exempt organizations as partners and to lessors of real or personal property to such partnerships.

The tax-exempt entity leasing provisions have a direct and significant impact on the structure and implementation of joint ventures involving tax-exempt hospitals. Unless properly structured to avoid their being applied by the IRS, the reduction of tax benefits to the taxable entities involved in such joint ventures is likely to increase the cost of the venture, in tax terms, to its participants.

WRAP-UP

Tax planning is an essential aspect of any hospital-physician joint venture. At a minimum, properly structuring the timing and amount of tax benefits in a joint venture will have a significant impact on its economic performance and the after-tax returns to the participants. In addition, proper tax planning at the outset may avoid bad business or financial decisions that need to be restructured.

Finally, tax-exempt joint-venture participants need to be especially concerned about the impact of their participation on their tax-exempt status. They also should take advantage of the opportunities to minimize the incidence of unrelated business income tax on their distributive shares of profits.

Chapter 6

Legal Issues and Joint Ventures*

> AND SO EACH VENTURE IS A NEW BEGINNING . . .
>
> *T. S. Eliot*

*Based on material contributed by Gary W. Eiland of the law firm of Wood, Lucksinger & Epstein, Houston.

HIGHLIGHTS

- Internal and External Parameters
- Types of Structures for Joint Ventures: Definitions and Characteristics
- Business corporations—Advantages and Disadvantages
- Not-for-Profit Corporations

6

> **JOINT VENTURING DEFINED**
>
> A joint venture is an association of two or more persons to carry out a single business for profit. It is usually, but not necessarily, limited to a single transaction.

INTERNAL AND EXTERNAL PARAMETERS

Defining a joint venture, and simply determining to establish one, does not necessarily a joint venture make. There are serious legal and social considerations to be taken into account before you sign on the proverbial bottom line, such as the following.

Political Considerations

Any joint venture brings into play internal politics and relationships. Entities to be taken into consideration before forming a joint venture are the hospitals board, the medical staff, the administration, the personnel, and, for many organizations and institutions, labor unions.

External Politics and Marketing

Public opinion, local government restrictions such as zoning and subdivision regulations, health ordinances, state mandates such as certificates of need, indigent care requirements, and employer concerns, such as health care coalitions and competing alternatives in employee benefit plans, HMOs, PPOs—all are to be taken in account before organizing a joint venture.

Power and Authority Factors

Potential joint ventures must take into consideration constitutional constraints on:

- owning stock in a corporation or association
- making loans or contributing anything of value to a corporation, association, or individual
- extending credit to a corporation, association, or individual
- proprietary ventures.

There also are statutory restrictions, involving a hospital district with taxing authority, a hospital authority without taxing authority, a city-owned hospital, a county hospital.

There are significant political questions as to reorganizations designed to avoid those constitutional or statutory restrictions.

- the public's perception that the reorganization somehow will steal the hospital from the public; and
- the concern that health care will be inaccessible to indigents.

Debt Financing Restrictions

Constraints involving financing the joint venture through bonds or other debt include:

- "black hole" default provisions
- restrictions on asset transfers
- permitted encumbrance and investment limitations
- maintenance of required financial ratios

TYPES OF STRUCTURES FOR JOINT VENTURES

General Partnership

The characteristics of a general partnership may vary from state to state, but most states have adopted the Uniform Partnership Act (UPA).

> The Uniform Partnership Act definition: "A partnership is an association of two or more persons to carry on as co-owners a business for profit."

The characteristics of such a partnership are as follows:

- The partnership can buy and sell real property.
- All partners are considered agents of the partnership, and the actions of any one partner within the course of the partnership business bind the partnership.
- Joint and several liability provides that all partners are jointly and severally liable for partnership liabilities in regards to wrongful acts or omissions of any partner made in the ordinary course of business. Depending on the circumstances, this can include not only negligence but also intentional torts and breaches of trust.
- Joint and several liability exposes each partner individually for the entire partnership's liability. A partner can be sued personally and individually, and such debt and judgment may be obtained against fewer than all the partners.
- Joint and several liability has tax implications for tax-exempt charitable organization that places their individual assets at risk in a joint venture with private individuals or corporation.
- Joint liability makes the partners jointly liable for all other debts and obligations of the partnership.

Advantages of a General Partnership

- It can be formed with little formality.
- It is very flexible.
- Its tax benefits flow through to the partners.
- It eliminates double taxation, such as on dividends.
- It may increase the ability to make offerings of tax-exempt securities.
- It has no organization fees or taxes.
- Its profits and losses may be allocated disproportionately except under certain circumstances.
- It requires no minimum capitalization.
- It gives all partners the right to participate in management.
- Its tax deductions may exceed the amount of cash invested.

Disadvantages of a General Partnership

- Its partners are exposed to legal liabilities.
- Its partnership form may complicate governance.
- It lacks continuity of interest.
- Its partnership rights generally are not transferable.
- Its income is taxed to each partner when earned, not when it is distributed generally.
- It may be treated by the IRS as an association and taxed as a corporation.
- It may come under unincorporated associations taxes in some states.
- Its partners owe fiduciary duties to each other.

Uses of General Partnerships

General partnerships are useful in a number of types of situations for hospitals and/or physicians and physician groups (Figure 6-1).

Limited Partnerships

> A limited partnership is a partnership formed by two or more persons, having as members one or more general partners and one or more limited partners. The limited partners shall not be bound by the obligations of the partnerships.

The characteristics of a limited partnership include the following:

- Limited partners have limited liability, so they can invest in limited partnership in a manner similar to shareholders in a corporation.
- Limited partners must not exercise control of the business if they are to avoid the liability as a general partner.
- Limited partners have the right to assign their proprietary interest in the firm without the consent of other members and without leading to the dissolution of the partnership.

Who May Become a Limited Partner?

Unlike UPA, the ULPA does not explicitly include corporation in its definition of "persons." Case lost supporting corporation right to be

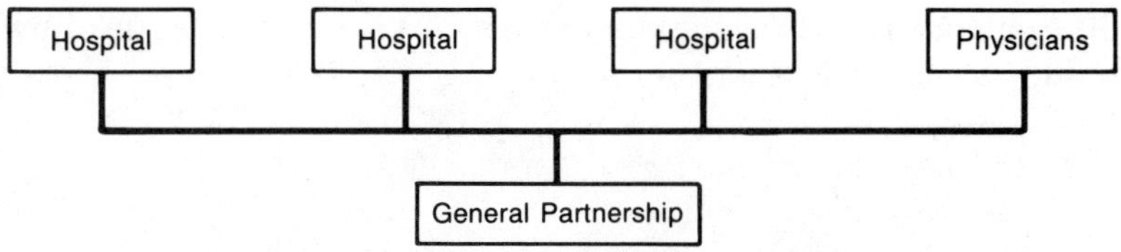

- Partnership agreement
- Control/management
- General equality of partners
- Activities: hospital support services (laundry, data processing, lab, maintenance, CAT-scan, area health development, wellness, sports)

Hospital Venture with Physician Group

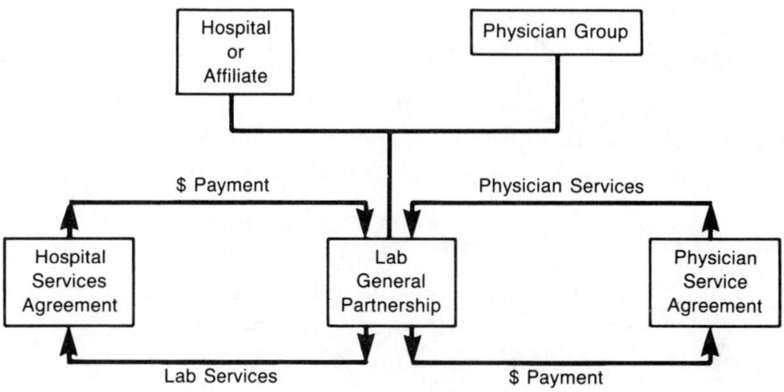

- Partnership agreement
- Control/management
- Equality of interests
- Activities: sports medicine clinic, ambulatory care, commercial lab

Partnership Agreement

- Equality of decision making/profit sharing
- Small number of partners
- Physician requirements
  1. active practice maintained
  2. geographic limitations
  3. convenant not to compete
  4. retirement or death, sale of shares
  5. physician services agreement
- Hospital requirements
  1. purchase of services
  2. asset contributions (land, facilities, development support)
  3. furnishing of services (ancillary health care, accounting, billing and collection, maintenance)

Figure 6-1 Uses of a General Partnership

limited partner. However, statutory provisions in some states do allow corporations to be limited partners.

Limited Partner's Contribution and Liability

In general, the limited partner must make a contribution to the capital of the business, while the general partner does not. The character of the contribution may be cash or other property, but not services. This contribution must be paid prior to the formation of the partnership.

The general rule regarding liability is that limited partners are not personally liable for partnership debts and obligations beyond the amount of their contribution.

An example of the use of a limited partnership is presented in Figure 6-2.

Advantages of a Limited Partnership

- It offers tax benefits to investors.
- It makes possible equity participation by more investors.
- It reduces the business risk to each limited partner.

Disadvantages of a Limited Partnership

- Its limited partners cannot manage the entity, or participate in its management.
- It wants the investors' equity, not their interference.

Business Corporations

Advantages of a Business Corporation

- It limits in liability.
- Its stock generally is freely transferable.
- It offers financing flexibility.
- It is managed by a board of directors rather than by the stockholders generally, but shareholders generally have more control than a limited partner.
- It includes no fiduciary duties among stockholders or between stockholders and the company.
- Its profits are shared in proportion to stock ownership.
- It has continuity of existence.
- Intercorporation dividend exclusion

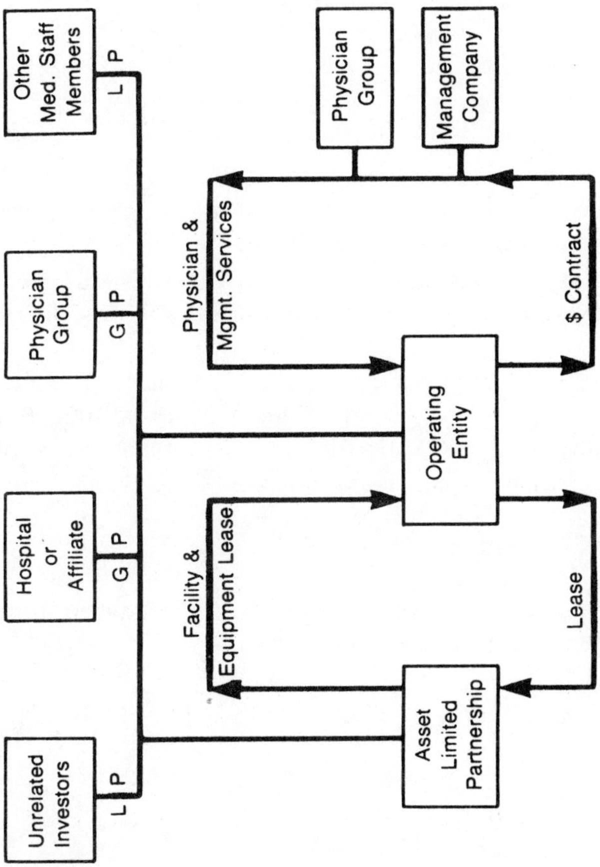

Figure 6-2 Uses of a Limited, Partnership

NOTE: LP = limited partner
GP = general partner.

Disadvantages of a Business Corporation

- It cannot be formed without formalities.
- It must pay initial and annual fees and taxes.
- There must be formal requirements for notice.
- It is subject to statutory minimum capitalization requirements.
- It subjects shareholders to double taxation.
- Its power and authority are limited in some states.

Uses of a Business Corporation

A business corporation is valuable in a number of particular situations, such as:

- for ventures where few capital assets are involved, such as service organizations and home health systems
- for nonprofit hospital transactions where tax-exempt status is not attainable, such as multihospital ventures, labs, laundries, data processing, etc.
- for venturers where ease of management and/or limited liability are desired, such as situations in which there is no willing general partner, or a corporate form is desired for management and control.
- for ventures in which tax considerations are not relevant.

The Not-for-Profit Corporation

In this category, the rules of the game generally are the same as those for business corporations, with these exceptions:

- They contain limitations on private inurement and nonexempt activity.
- They generally pay little or no taxes, state or federal.
- They may be limited in purpose.
- They can benefit from tax-exempt gifts.
- They may be eligible for special grants and loans.
- They may have restrictions on incentive programs.
- They may have limitations on political activity.
- Their nonprofit tax-exempt status may be jeopardized by participation depending on the joint-venture transactions.

WRAP-UP

This has been a brief description of some of the legal organizational structures possible in joint-venturing. For a more detailed discussion, see Appendix A on Alternative Legal Models for Joint Ventures.

> RED FLAGS
>
> - Political considerations can make or break any deal that your hospital may venture into. Politics do count.
> - There will be a power struggle. Decide up front that you want to win.

Chapter 7

Solid Market Research Will Ensure Success

...MEN HERE...COME TO BELIEVE...THAT THE BEST TEST OF TRUTH IS THE POWER OF THE THOUGHT TO GET ITSELF ACCEPTED IN THE COMPETITION OF THE MARKET...

Justice Oliver Wendell Holmes Jr.

FUNDAMENTALLY, THERE ARE ONLY TWO WAYS OF COORDINATING THE ECONOMIC IDEAS OF MILLIONS. ONE IS CENTRAL DIRECTIONS INVOLVING THE USE OF COERCION—THE TECHNIQUE OF THE ARMY AND OF THE MODERN TOTALITARIAN STATE. THE OTHER IS VOLUNTARY COOPERATION OF INDIVIDUALS—THE TECHNIQUE OF THE MARKETPLACE.

Milton Friedman

HIGHLIGHTS

- Definition of Market Research
- What Market Research Can Do for a Joint Venture
- How to Start the Market Research Process
- Components of Business Plan/Market Research Vehicle
- Steps to Go Through in Evaluating and Selecting a Joint-Venture Opportunity
- Establishing Goals
- Keeping the Physicians Firmly in Mind
- Benefits Provided by Physician Co-Venturers
- How and What to Look At in Considering a Joint Venture
- The Market Audit
- Market Segmentation: Identifying Customer or Homogenous Groups—Case Studies
- Market Segments of the Female Health Care Customer
- Finding Nontraditional Consumer Markets
- Different Types of Demographic Analyses
- Methods for Ascertaining Market Information

7

WHAT IS MARKET RESEARCH?

Basically, market research is a feedback system that lets management know what is happening in the surrounding environment. Management research provides information on the organization's competition, its target audience, its members and clients, alternative advertising schemes, and the probability of a new idea's success or failure.

> Market research is "the systematic and objective gathering, recording, and analyzing of information relevant to the solution of problems in the field of marketing."
>
> *John P. Dickson and Sarah S. Dickson*

WHAT CAN MARKET RESEARCH DO FOR A JOINT VENTURE?

1. Market research can reduce the probability of failure.
2. Market research can assist the joint venture in understanding and planning for present and future markets.
3. Market research can assist the joint venture in developing products and services that are likely to succeed in the given market place.

4. Market research can provide a system of monitoring the success and/or failure of the joint venture.
5. Market research can bring to light new products and services and new ways of marketing them that may not have been apparent immediately.

HOW TO START THE MARKET RESEARCH PROCESS

One of the best tools for starting the market research process is that old standby and friend in need, the business plan. When you break out a business plan into its major component parts, you will find that they are identical to the component parts that a good market research program should deliver.

BUSINESS PLAN/RESEARCH COMPONENTS

These components include such factors as conducting an assessment of the business environment, determining how the process will be organized and operated, the financial elements, and finally the actual marketing itself.

Environmental Assessment

- demands of the market
- market segments in the immediate area being serviced
- demographics in the immediate area being serviced
- consumer behavior not only of physicians but also of potential patients
- suppliers involved in the joint venture
- analysis of competition to the joint venture
- access and availability by the various users to the joint venture.

Organization

- legal components and considerations of the joint venture
- tax considerations, in both for-profit and not-for-profit entities
- any corporate reorganization that may be necessary to ensure the success of the joint venture

- the nature and product and services of the joint venture itself, as well as its organizational structure.

Operations

- initial products the joint venture will provide to the marketplace—in the case of hospital joint ventures, this also will include service-related products
- proposed products that in the near or distant future the joint venture might offer to the marketplace
- staffing and personnel requirements ensure the success of the joint venture
- equipment requirements
- the facility—description, accessibility, space requirements—that the joint venture will need.

Financial

- service projections
- revenue assumptions and pro forma statements
- fixed and variable costs
- cash-flow predictions, perhaps through comparisons with similar joint ventures already in existence
- first-year departmental budgets
- pro forma income statements to assess the feasibility of the project and its direction
- pro forma balance sheets.

Marketing

- the objectives of the market plan
- strategies to implement the objectives
- a system for product and service development through the joint venture
- promotion, including advertising, direct mail, and other promotional devices, to ensure the success of the delivery of the venturer's product or service
- implementation of the marketing plan.

These are the critical components of market research, as they are of a business plan, and must be highly developed before a joint venture should be undertaken.

STEPS IN SELECTING A JOINT VENTURE

Establishing Goals

Every hospital organization has a mission. Whether it's written or simply understood, a mission or reason for existence exists. Often, this is outlined in the organization's long-range strategic plan. An essential first step in evaluating joint venture opportunities is to recognize the strategic mission of the hospital or either of the coventurers.

> Not all opportunities, no matter how sound a business investment, will provide a good fit with the organizational mission. For example, a Catholic hospital would not be willing to enter a joint venture with a physician group to develop an ambulatory surgery center if the physicians intended to perform sterilizations and abortions. A less obvious example would be for a not-for-profit organization whose mission is focused on charitable activities to consider entry into commercial ventures. The dissonance created by a venture inconsistent with an organization's mission can have an adverse impact on board members and community relations that far outweighs the expected benefits.
>
> *Daniel J. Sullivan*

Assuring the Joint Venture Will Be a Good Fit

Here are several criteria to consider in evaluating whether or not the particular joint venture under consideration will fit with the hospital's organizational goals.

> - Will the venture build on existing organizational strengths?
> - Does the venture reduce identified weaknesses in the current organization?

- Does the venture minimize or maximize competitive threats to the organization?

WARNING

A major failing of many joint-venture projects is that the business strategy is defined incompletely.

Establishing Expectations

Hospital XYZ is evaluating a proposal from a group of staff radiologists to open a free-standing diagnostic imaging center at a site away from the hospital. The physicians are willing to give the hospital a 50 percent ownership position in the center. The physicians will have exclusive rights to read films, for which they will be paid a percentage of gross revenue. How can the hospital determine whether this particular investment opportunity is one it should pursue?

The hospital must define its goals or expectations for the life of the joint venture. The hospital should always keep in mind its underlying goals. It should not, in the heat of negotiations, compromise in an effort to do the deal, with a devastatingly drastic result to itself.

PRELIMINARY ASSESSMENT

At the very least, a preliminary assessment of a joint-venture project should include:

- the range of services
- the type of equipment required
- the general location
- the physicians' interest and needs
- the target market

Keeping the Physicians Firmly in Mind

Determining the physicians' interest and needs is particularly important when considering joint ventures for health-related services, particularly those outside the hospital. These services—such as urgent care, ambulatory surgery, diagnostic testing, and primary care—may in fact end up competing directly with physicians.

If there is significant opposition to a project by a medical staff, this could result in hostility from staff members and decreased morale for the hospital. Too often, hospitals and their physicians find themselves on opposite sides in certificate-of-need proceedings, or duplicating services in a single market.

Considering physicians' attitudes, and involving doctors early in planning processes, can turn an area of weakness into one of strength. Physicians who are informed and consulted on a hospital's plan can provide a valuable source of support. At the same time, they can offer important insights into the definition and location of new services.

BENEFITS OF PHYSICIAN CO-VENTURERS

If the physician partners also are users of the new service, utilization levels can be reached more easily than if the hospital has to market the services outside to doctors with whom it is not associated.

Physicians can provide a source of capital to fund the project.

LET'S GET REALLY PICKY, NOW

Industry Examination

Now let's take a close look at the consumers of the joint venture:

- Is there a referral process?
- How do consumers even get in to use the service?
- Why would consumers use the joint venture?
- What are the existing referral networks, if any?

If you don't know how you're going to get your customers, you may not get your customers at all.

The Money Question

Ask yourself these following questions about reimbursement for the services or the product that the joint venture will offer:

- Is the service going to be covered by major insurance companies?

- Are these services desirable to preferred provider organizations and health maintenance organizations?
- What are the expectations for reimbursement in the future?

More Money Factors To Consider

- Are significant startup costs or major capital investments required?
- Are specific types of expertise required that are not readily available and that will have to be purchased?
- Are low-cost providers of this product or service already in the marketplace who will form a formidable opposition?

> **WARNING**
>
> **If you don't know the answers to these questions, don't get into the game.**

LOOK AT THE SIMPLEST THINGS FIRST

In defining the area that your joint venture will be servicing, it's important to understand the simplest things, such as:

- How are the people who will be the end users of the products or services distributed?
- What are the transportation routes?
- What are the barriers to transportation in the area?
- How long does it take people from the outermost fringes of your market to get to your joint venture?

If your doctors and your clients or patients can't get together quickly, easily, with lots of parking and few hassles, the venture will not succeed.

DEMOGRAPHICS ARE IMPORTANT

Once you know where you want to locate the joint venture, make sure that the demographic composition of the area will support it. There is no sense in putting in a woman's clinic in an area that has few women. It also makes a great deal of sense to provide cardiovascular fitness centers in an area that is heavily populated by executives who are very conscious of their cardiovascular fitness needs.

Be very careful that you know who lives in the market area that you're going to be supplying and that you know exactly what it is that they want and will pay for.

COMPETITION, COMPETITION, COMPETITION

> Entry into a new service requires consideration of the competition in the expected service area. At the outset, the hospital must identify all competitors and map the location of each within the target market. In identifying competitors, it is necessary to look not only at those providing identical services but also at those who provide similar or substitute services. As an illustration: If a hospital is proposing to construct an urgent care center, it should consider not only other urgent care centers, but also primary care clinics with extended hours and hospital emergency centers.
>
> *Daniel J. Sulliven*

Here's what to look for when you're assessing the competition—you might call it a market audit (Exhibit 7-1):

- ownership and control of the organization with which you are competing
- the scope of the services provided by the competition
- the historical utilization level of the competition
- the market share of your competitor
- plans your competitor may have to expand or diversify services
- existing entrenched referral networks.

MINI WRAP-UP

Don't become frustrated. The market research segment of setting up a joint venture is perhaps the most tedious, labor-intensive, and boring component of the entire process. However, as with any other project, the more time and the more care you spend in the preparation stages, the

Exhibit 7-1 The Market Audit

	Inside	Outside
How many patients are there?		
Which categories of care do they use?		
Where are they located?		
Where do they go for what kinds of care?		
How do they become patients?		
How do they feel—		
About the hospital?		
About its competition?		
What do they perceive as the hospital's—		
Strengths?		
Weaknesses?		
How do they perceive other hospitals?		
What factors influence their decision—		
To seek care?		
To choose a physician?		
To choose a hospital?		
What would they change about the hospital?		
What would they do if the hospital changed?		
What specific new services might they use if these were made available?		
Under what circumstances would they use such services?		
How would they react if the hospital added them?		
What would happen if the hospital dropped some existing services?		
How many physicians are there?		
Where are they located?		
Which specialties do they offer?		
How many patients do they admit?		
What portion of these patients comes to the hospital?		
How do they feel—		
About the hospital?		
About its competition?		
What do they perceive as the hospital's—		
Strengths?		
Weaknesses?		
How do they perceive other hospitals?		
What factors influence their choice?		
What are their plans for the future?		
What would they change about the hospital?		
What would they do if the hospital changed?		
What new services might they use?		
Under what circumstances would they use such services?		
How would they react if the hospital added them?		
What would happen if the hospital dropped some existing services?		

Source: Reprinted from *Journal of Health Care Marketing,* Vol. 1, No. 1, with permission of American Marketing Association, © Winter 1980–81.

more successful you will be in the delivery stage. So remember: A little extra time spent up front can reap you great rewards on the final bottom line.

MARKET SEGMENTATION

> Market segmentation refers to the process of delineating or identifying a customer group or groups with homogeneous or similar needs that the joint venture or business must satisfy.

WOMEN AS A MARKET FOR JOINT VENTURES

An example of market segmentation in joint ventures is women. It is a given, and has been since the feminist revolution of the 1960s and 1970s, that women can be viewed as a single homogeneous market within the larger health care consumer market.

However, before setting up a joint venture that caters exclusively to a female population, certain audit steps should be taken in order to better understand the target market. At the outset, it is important to understand factors that influence a woman's choice of a health care provider.

Health Concern

Women are very conscious about the importance of their contacts with a variety of different health providers. By and large, women need to trust and feel confident in their physicians, and are more likely to question their prescriptions than are men.

Pattern of Health Service Use

It is essential to determine the pattern of health service use, which means the number of contacts that a woman would have with her health care provider or clinic. It must be understood that women also play the dominant role in selecting a physician for other members of the family, particularly children.

This is an important consideration when looking at the overall market that women represent. Women on their own constitute but one small segment; however, as they influence the health purchasing decisions of others, they are a much expanded market.

Women's Process of Choosing a Provider

Women between the ages of 17 and 35 or 40 tend to be very confident when they make decisions about who will provide their and their family's health care. Those over 40 are less confident and tend not to change physicians or clinics easily. This is an important consideration when starting joint venture that will cater specifically to women.

If your joint venture is in a demographic area that contains large numbers of younger women, chances are they can be convinced to switch to your facility; if, on the other hand, the majority of women in the area are older, you will have a much harder sell.

Market Segments in Female Health Care

There are several identifiable segments into which women health care shoppers can be divided:

- *The traditional:* These seek health care when they are sick or require a checkup. They do what they think should be done that is consistent with how they have been brought up.
- *Family-Centered:* These enthusiastically support and promote family well-being. They enjoy the role as family health care decisionmakers. They promote an active, aggressive family and take pride in the responsibility for family health.
- *Sports-Oriented:* These are concerned with the performance of their own bodies. They're oriented toward competition. They're aggressive, independent, and seek treatment when their health interferes with their performance.
- *Wellness/Wholeness:* These are interested in nutrition, longevity, and enhancing health. Their focus is on the total human experience—mind, spirit, and body. They seek both general and specific health-related information and tend to prefer alternatives to traditional medical treatment where possible.
- *The Avoiders:* These minimize contact with health care services because of distrust, fear, disinterest, or lack of financial resources. They promote an active, aggressive family and take pride in the responsibility for family health.

To meet the needs of a female-oriented market with a female-oriented joint-venture product or service, these areas must be studied carefully and included in market research. Make sure you're not offering apples to someone who really enjoys oranges much more.

NONTRADITIONAL CONSUMER MARKETS

It seems almost too obvious to state that there are different markets for health care: men, women, children, the elderly, the young, the sick, the well. This is just slicing the health care pie in different ways.

However, within those general categories of market are hidden or nontraditional consumer groups. Following is a type of profile or survey that a joint venture can adapt in order to identify hidden markets for its services.

PROFILE OF CONSUMER ATTITUDES

Section 1: Information for Choices

- I trust my doctor's opinion about hospitals.
- It would be nice to have a consumer rating service for hospitals.
- It's important to ask around, to learn a hospital's reputation.
- Hospitals should advertise their services and rates.
- It's best to find someone who's been there before choosing a hospital.
- Hospitals should survey patients to ascertain their feelings.

Section 2: Health Care Costs

- Costs would go down if hospitals were run like a business.
- Hospitals don't really try to keep costs down.
- Costs would go up if hospitals start to advertise.
- Costs would go down if hospitals were to share services.
- Hospital costs seem to be rising for no real reason.
- Government should be more active in lowering the cost of hospital charges.
- The best way to lower hospital costs would be to close some hospitals.
- The saying, "You get what you pay for," is definitely true in medicine.

- Health care is big business.

Section 3: Hospital Systems

- Some hospitals are better than others.
- I prefer a hospital with my religious affiliation.
- The best hospitals have a wide range of services.
- New teaching hospitals usually have all the services you need.
- Most hospitals are alike.
- Hospitals associated with medical schools usually are better.
- There are not enough hospitals to care for the people who need them.
- People's faith in hospitals has gone down dramatically in the last few years.
- All hospitals should offer special services such as diet workshops and stop-smoking programs.
- All hospitals should have plans for low-income consumers.
- I have had good feelings about the hospitals I've been in.
- I feel that most hospitals have high ethical standards.

Section 4: Time

- It is easier to go to a hospital when I have a problem than to get an appointment with a doctor.
- It's best just to go to the closest hospital in an emergency.
- I always choose the hospital that is closest to where I live for my medical needs.

By adapting this survey to the needs of your own joint venture, and polling your demographic area, you will begin to develop a profile of the likely consumers, both overt and covert, both obvious and hidden, who might become users of the various services and products that your joint venture offers.

DEMOGRAPHIC ANALYSIS

There are several ways to obtain a correct demographic analysis of the market you hope to serve. The method you choose depends on the amount of time *or* money you have to spend.

If you have the time—and not a lot of money—a trip to a large public library is a good beginning. Ask the reference librarian to show you the data from the U.S. Census Bureau and other reports from agencies such as the state health department, local planning councils, and chambers of commerce. Some HSAs also provide low cost demographic information.

If your hospital or company has a library or research center with "online" computer services, Donnelley Demographics—a database of demographic and other marketing information—is an inexpensive and time-saving option. A four-page profile of a ZIP code area, city, county, or other subdivision costs about $12. For more information, call Donnelley at (203)965-5454.

Many colleges, universities, and public libraries offer data base searching for marketing research on a cost recovery basis.

AMA Market Area Profile (MAP) Service

Some of the key questions asked and answered by the AMA Market Area Profile Service are:

- How many people reside in the area?
- Is it a stable population base or is the growth rate expected to increase or decline significantly?
- What are the characteristics (age, sex, income) of the resident population?
- Are these characteristics expected to change in the next five years?
- What is the level of demand for medical specialties in this area now? In the future?
- How many other physicians or hospitals are located in the area? How old are they? What are their medical specialties?
- What is the extent of the potential referral base?
- Are hospital facilities adequate?
- What are the medical staff characteristics in the area?

You must be a licensed physician or a registered medical student to order AMA Market Area Profile Reports. You also must be able to define accurately the place or area you want to study. There are two ways that you can define your market area: you may specify a Ring Study or a Geographic Area Study.

Ring Study

A Ring Study is defined as a circle centered on a specific point that is a street intersection. You must be able to specify the radius in number of miles—the distance from the site to the periphery of the ring—and the specific street intersection that you are using as a center point. The radius of the ring can be any number of miles; however, unless it is an extremely dense area, yours should be five miles or more.

> A Ring Study is an especially useful type of analysis where you have a specific office or hospital site, either existing or planned, since it permits you to precisely define the surrounding service area.

In specifying a particular radius, it is important to remember that you want to include only the area from which you could reasonably expect to draw patients.

Geographic Area Study

If you do not have a specific hospital or office site in mind, but instead are interested in learning more about the demographic and health resource profile of a general area, you may request reports for either postal zip code, city or town, or county. In requesting such reports, however, it is important to keep in mind that the more specific you can be in defining your area of study, the more useful the MAP reports will be.

Therefore, if you are interested in a particular part of a metropolitan area, you should specify a particular zip code rather than the entire city or country. In rural areas, on the other hand, town (or even county) analysis may be appropriate. In short, in defining your area of study you should consider where your patients will be drawn from.

If you could reasonably expect them to travel from throughout the county to get to your hospital or office, county analysis may be helpful; if they might come from the entire city or town, that level of analysis may be indicated; and if they are likely to come from one or more particular zip codes, that may be the most appropriate area.

To order these reports, contact the Department of Physician Practice Service, The American Medical Association, 535 North Dearborn Street, Chicago, Ill. 60610.

The spectrum of demographic products and services is constantly broadening, with computerized "mapping" and customized phone surveys becoming popular—and expensive—tools for planning. A good way to monitor demographic trends is by reading *American Demographics,* a monthly magazine, that also publishes a "shopping list" of demographic services. A catalog of their publications and subscription information can be ordered by calling (800)828-1133.

ASCERTAINING MARKET INFORMATION

- Questionnaires sent out to the local population and to physicians who will be participating in the venture
- Personal interviews
- Telephone interviews
- Direct-mail marketing surveys
- Focus groups
- Advertising testing

WRAP-UP

The solid market research that you do, either alone or through consultants and other participants, will enable you to better plan a successful joint venture, and may open up new products and services that you hadn't even dreamed of. As noted earlier, this is the preparation stage for the joint venture, and it is critical.

RED FLAGS

- Don't guess that you know about market research. Find out before you form a venture.
- Don't delegate market research to a member of your own staff. Get outside, expert input.
- Don't massage the business plan along yourself from concept to implementation if you want to succeed. You can't do it all alone.

Chapter 8

Cautions and Pitfalls

> HASTE IN EVERY BUSINESS BRINGS FAILURES.
>
> *Herodotus*

HIGHLIGHTS

- The Business Plan as a Map of Success
- The Time Factor
- The Big Risk: Failure
- Who's to Blame for Failure
- Step-by-Step Guide to the Business Plan

8

Fundamentally, a joint venture is a business deal. Except for the individuals' chemistry and their different personalities, business deals fail (or get into trouble) because a sound business is not understood, not developed, and not followed. The individual group or institution entering a joint venture must take the elements of a business plan seriously.

Properly done, a business plan will cover the entire range of business activities, from conception and planning to making the first critical sale or seeing the first customer/patient. Effective business plans look at the following elements.

- what the environment is
- how the business will operate
- how it should be organized and function
- what the financial demands and rewards are
- what marketing plan has been devised, including objectives and new product development

The risks or pitfalls are in poor planning and in poor execution of the initial business plan.

THE BUSINESS PLAN AS A MAP FOR SUCCESS

Why You Need a Business Plan

The process of creating a business plan forces the venture to take a realistic, objective, and unemotional or detached look at the entire business. Why is it so important to see the venture as a whole? Most people who have business ideas deal with them haphazardly. Putting a plan together and writing down specifics not only gives the venturers a chance to see the business as it's being created but allows them to see the business from the outside, like the astronauts saw the earth as they circled the stratosphere.

A finished business plan is very useful because it becomes an operating tool that will assist the venture in managing the business and work toward its success. The final, completed plan is the chief instrument for communicating ideas to others: business people, bankers, partners, etc. If you seek financing for the venture, the plan becomes the basis of a loan proposal.

A business plan also marks the critical difference between venturers who simply have an idea and those who can make money on the idea. Once an idea is put on paper, it has a certain element of reality to it. And it is that reality that then can be translated into dollars and a solid black bottom line.

WARNING

It is imperative that venturers do your own business plan. You can hire help, you can hire typists, you can hire clerical advisers, you can hire legal advisers and tax advisers. But you yourself as the venturers must write the plan simply because it allows you to understand the business from its very conception through every stage and will help you succeed with it once it is implemented.

If you don't develop your own business plan step by step, you will never know all the little ins and outs.

A business plan, essentially, is a key to a business, and once you turn the key, all kinds of other things might pop out at you.

If you are not the one who has developed the plan single-handedly, you will miss much of those ins and outs and little twists and turnings in the business, and will not have as great a chance of succeeding.

The Time Factor is Important

A business plan is like a fresh head of lettuce. If it's not developed quickly, used, and implemented, it wilts. An idea is only as good as the moment in time in which it was conceived and developed. If you wait too long, the entire parade may well pass you by. So if you have an idea for a venture, start on it now, this very minute.

THE BIG RISK: FAILURE

Dun and Bradstreet reports that small businesses or small joint ventures have a very high failure rate. If you are aware of the reasons for failure when you work through your business plan, you will be able to eliminate much of them through careful attention to details and planning. Here are some of those reasons small businesses and co-ventures fail.

- Insufficient control over costs and quality of product
- Ineffective pricing
- Poor customer/patient relations
- A poor public image
- Inadequate relations with suppliers
- Poor management, or the inability to reach decisions and act on them at once
- Lack of key personnel
- Reluctance to seek professional assistance
- Lack of careful tax planning
- Lower-than-expected sales
- Poor training of staff in key positions
- Inability to deal effectively with competition
- Poor planning of market trends and demographics
- Inadequate cash flow
- Insufficient startup or working capital
- Lack of financial data instantly

Who's To Blame for Failure?

The reasons given for business failures are as varied as those giving the opinions. Some blame politics or supply-side economics. Some blame interest rates. Some blame unemployment. Some blame high budget deficits. Some blame low rates of savings and investments.

However, the two key reasons for failure of any small business or coventure are very simply these:

1. failure to pay attention to every single detail
2. failure to explore every single opportunity that the venture itself presents.

THE BUSINESS PLAN: A STEP-BY-STEP DO-IT-YOURSELF PROGRAM

1. The Cover Page

- Name of venture and status
- Address
- Phone number
- List of principals
- Logo, if any
- Submitted to (for financing only)

2. The Executive Summary

The executive summary should be one page, no more. It is a synopsis of the entire business plan. Even if your business plan reaches 50 or 60 pages, you must be able to boil down the main components into one or two paragraphs on the Executive Summary page.

The Executive Summary should state the nature of the business, the market it will serve, the need for such a business, and its potential for growth and financial success.

3. Purpose (One Page, for Financing)

- Company name and type
- Amount of money needed
- How the money will be used
- Effect of money on the business

3. Purpose (One Page for Nonfinancial Plan)

- Company name and type
- Goals or policies of the plan

- How the plan will be implemented
- Effect of the policies on the business

4. Table of Contents

5. The Business Plan Proper

a. Environmental Assessment

- demand for the business
- market segments
- demographics
- consumer behavior
- suppliers
- competition
- access and availability to the service or business
- other factors

b. Operations

- initial products
- start-up time
- proposed products
- developmental time
- staffing and management
- policies for dealing with physicians and medical staff
- equipment requirements
- facility requirements
- day-to-day problems
- other obstacles/considerations

c. Organization

- legal structure
- tax considerations
- corporation reorganization
- joint venture types

d. Service Projections

- revenue assumptions
- fixed variable costs

- cash flow
- first-year departmental budget
- pro forma income statement
- pro forma balance sheet

e. Marketing

- objectives
- strategies
- product/service development
- promotion
- advertising
- implementation

f. Supporting Information

- resumes and curricula vitae
- letters of intent
- purchase orders
- letters of recommendation
- job descriptions
- newspaper and magazine clippings
- any other additional relevant information supporting the venture

RED FLAGS

- The biggest pitfall is poor planning
- The second biggest pitfall is poor execution of the original business plan.
- The ventures must beware of delegating out the job of doing the business plan. There are many things that other experts can do for you—the business plan is not one of them
- Two turkeys do not an eagle make. Remember that and don't try to force a business arrangement if it isn't really there.
- Don't bring in all the experts too early. More business deals have been "detailed" to death and oblivion by overly cautious accountants and lawyers. Get your act together first, then bring in the troops.

Part II

Joint Venture Partners

Chapter 9

Hospitals with Hospitals

THE MADMAN'S RULE

ANY VENTURE INTO A NEW AREA OF TECHNOLOGY WILL COST THREE AND A HALF TIMES THE ORIGINAL ESTIMATE BECAUSE OF UNFORESEEN DIFFICULTIES.

Quoted in *The New York Times,* June 3, 1972

HIGHLIGHTS

- Components of a Good Fit
- A Case Study: Obstetrics
- A Case Study: For-Profit Chains and Teaching Hospitals
- Joint Venture Work Sheets

9

In the health care environment of the late 1980s, a natural but still uncomfortable alliance among hospitals through joint venturing was emerging. In the so-called "good old days" hospitals served a defined community, they duplicated services, and they pulled their patients from a market unconcerned wtih diagnosis related groups (DRGs), health maintenance organizations (HMOs) and preferred provider organizations (PPOs). That of course has changed. Hospitals now are finding themselves in direct competition with one another for patients who suddenly have many more health care options.

> **One response to this situation is for hospitals to take a critical look at their fellows and determine which ones would make the least threatening and most satisfying bedfellows.**

How do you as the hospital administrator select the best fit for your hospital when co-venturing with another?

COMPONENTS OF 'FIT'

- **Is your mission the same as the prospective joint venture partner's?**
- **Is your long-term set of objectives similar?**
- **Are your short-term goals compatible?**
- **Are the markets you serve almost the same?**

- Are there areas of technical/equipment expertise that would clash?
- Are there potential staff conflicts?
- Are there areas of serious department duplications?
- Are there religious differences?
- Are there ethnic/demographic differences?

AREAS OF POTENTIAL JOINT VENTURES

A Case Study in Obstetrics*

Although three years ago [1977] a fire forced St. Joseph's Hospital to close its obstetrics department, care for expectant mothers became available through a new joint venture with St. Mary Hospital, 14 blocks away.

The project, which began January 18, 1980, allows women who normally would get prenatal and obstetric care at St. Joseph's to attend an OB clinic there that is run by St. Mary personnel. The women are taken to St. Mary for delivery. After the child is born, they are encouraged to return to St. Joseph's for postpartum care and pediatric services.

St. Mary rents the clinic to St. Joseph for $1 a year and provides half a dozen physicians and a dozen nurses and nurse practitioners. St. Mary also has a van and an ambulance to transport the pregnant women.

Ironing Out the Kinks

Transportation was the biggest obstacle to the program. Because St. Joseph's clients depend primarily on public transit, St. Mary Hospital "two trolley rides and a transfer away," was undesirable to neighborhood women before the joint venture provided transportation.

"Philadelphia is a large city, and certain streets become boundary lines" explained Sister Mary Anita CSSF, St. Joseph's administrator. "People don't cross

*Adapted from *Hospital Progress* (now *Health Progress*), Vol. 61, No. 10, pp. 22, 24, with permission of Catholic Health Association of the United States, © October 1980.

these boundaries to get health care. By sharing programs, we see a lot of patients who otherwise wouldn't get to either St. Joseph's or St. Mary's."

Setting Up the Payment Structure

Financial arrangement available to expectant mothers at St. Mary's include a $650 charge for the working poor, which is paid off over nine months, and state financing. Medicaid covers 90 percent of the program's patients. Care is free to those who cannot pay.

"We set up the time payment plan because paying is often important for the patient's personal dignity," said I. Donald Snook, Jr., administrator of St. Mary's Hospital. "However, the lack of money should not keep an unborn child from the gift of life."

Other Program Pluses

St. Mary also offers prenatal and parenting classes for St. Joseph mothers, including "Early Bird," offered in the first trimester and covering personal hygiene, diet, and exercise during pregnancy; courses in prepared childbirth, delivering by Caesarean section, and breast-feeding; and a refresher course for parents with other children that includes siblings.

The expectant mothers tour the St. Mary facilities before delivery. Since merging forces with St. Joseph's, St. Mary has renovated a birthing room with a trans-cultural motif to serve the multicultures of the inner city. An entire wall can be changed, allowing the laboring woman to chose an attractive environment reflecting her cultural heritage, Snook said.

Advertising and Promotion

The program was advertised by word of mouth and by a large sign outside St. Joseph's. In addition, brochures were delivered door to door within a ten-block radius of St. Joseph Hospital; posters and brochures went to neighborhood churches, community organizations, and stores; car cards were posted in trolleys that serve both hospitals; and a radio commercial was broadcast 21 times a week every other week for six weeks.

How It Worked

Since the start of the program, a dozen St. Joseph's women have delivered at St. Mary. About 50 more have registered for delivery within the year.

Decision To Share the Program

Licensed for 191 beds, St. Joseph's cut back to 161 after the fire damaged a medical-surgical wing. "We needed the extra space for medical-surgical use and for offices" said Sister Anita. "I had opposed closing the obstetrics service for moral and ethical reasons, but we were down to only eight deliveries a month, and that's not good utilization of 20 beds. Medical-surgical demand is always at capacity. The fire forced us to rethink."

Despite the fact that its number of deliveries was climbing rapidly, St. Mary still had the problem of possible health systems agency (HSA) intervention. St. Joseph's, which planned to open a new 178-bed hospital, decided not to add an OB service then because of HSA pressures.

After the decision to end OB services, St. Joseph's referred its maternity patients to other hospitals, primarily a nearby university medical center. St. Mary received few referrals. Snook, who developed the joint venture plans late in November 1979, says he was slow on the uptake.

"We've always been interested in sharing services, and the idea finally came to me when we were making our annual review of the hospital's long-range plan," he recalled. "It occurred to the planning committee that we have to go beyond the neighborhood. And if we're to reach out, we should not be in competition with others but be where there is a real need. St. Joseph's is the only one with the same mission. We're deeply committed to obstetrics here, so it didn't take us long to get on the phone to Sister Anita and do some fine tuning and orientation of their staff."

A Program Byproduct

A program byproduct is that St. Mary Hospital now could reach the HSA 1,000-baby requirement and thus not lose federal funding. Eight hundred babies were delivered there in the year ending June 30, 1980, and the additional 200 were to be delivered by St. Joseph's mothers.

> *Response*
>
> Response by the two hospitals' boards, staffs, and patients has been "100 percent supportive," both administrators agree. "I wish all my programs had so few problems," Snook said. "But then, we're dealing primarily with well people coming in for a joyful experience."

FOR-PROFIT CHAINS AND TEACHING HOSPITALS

According to a study by A.T. Kearney, Inc., a Chicago-based management consulting firm, teaching hospitals and for-profit hospital chains are increasing their joint-venture activities and looking at each other as workable partners.

The study analyzed the activities of 23 for-profit hospital chains. It found that five were potentially interested in linking with teaching hospitals, six actually had entered into formal relationships, and 12 had no plans for such affiliation. The affiliations most often identified were in acquisitions, lease management contracts, and program joint ventures.

WRAP-UP

Hospitals are natural allies in the war being waged in the health care industry and can stand strongly together against whatever assaults are launched by government and industry to reduce the costs of service.

CHECKLIST

JOINT VENTURE WITH ANOTHER HOSPITAL

Positives

1. Multiple services under one umbrella
2. Diversification of program base and offerings
3. Possibility of new program offerings such as substance abuse and women's clinics
4. Formation of HMOs and PPOs to capture and lock in client base
5. Ability to hire and maintain high-level technical personnel
6. Elimination of duplication of services

7. Ability to pursue economies of scale
8. Retention of market share

Negatives

1. Incompatibility of long-term goals and organizational mission
2. Friction between medical staffs
3. Loss of market share
4. Patient resistance to joint venture

Possible Partners and Services

List all compatible hospitals in your demographic area that might become co-ventureres

1. ______________________________

2. ______________________________

3. ______________________________

4. ______________________________

5. ______________________________

6. ______________________________

List all duplicate services provided within your market area in conflict with those of other nearby centers

Service 1 ______________________________

Service 2 ______________________________

Service 3 ______________________________

Service 4 ______________________________

Outline in detail services not currently being provided to your local consumers by any hospital in the immediate geographic area

____

____

____

Strengths

List the unique strengths of your hospital in order of priority and market perception

1. __________________ 4. __________________

2. __________________ 5. __________________

3. __________________ 6. __________________

Profile Analysis of Competitors

List in order of most critical competitor the hospitals in your market area and analyze which offer unique services that are not offered by your own facility or that are perceived to have programs superior to yours.

Hospital Competitor # 1

____

____

____

Hospital Competitor # 2

____

____

____

Hospital Competitor # 3

____

____

____

JOINT VENTURES WITH PHYSICIANS

Significant Developments

1. Changes in physician population
2. Changes in reimbursement
3. Increases in numbers of nonphysician practitioners
4. Increasingly competitive medical climate
5. Pressure from government and industry to reduce costs of medical services
6. HMOs and PPOs
7. More sophisticated health care consumers
8. Rapid development of high-technology diagnostic equipment
9. Wellness and fitness programs to supplement inpatient care

Chapter 10

Other Types of Joint Ventures

HIGHLIGHTS

- New Beginnings
- New Alternatives: The MeSH
- Development of a HEPP

10

HOSPITALS WITH DOCTORS

> THE TEST OF A FIRST-RATE INTELLIGENCE IS THE ABILITY TO HOLD TWO OPPOSED IDEAS IN MIND AT THE SAME TIME AND STILL RETAIN THE ABILITY TO FUNCTION.
>
> *F. Scott Fitzgerald*

> RUNYON'S LAW
>
> THE RACE IS NOT ALWAYS TO THE SWIFT, NOR THE BATTLE TO THE STRONG, BUT THAT'S THE WAY TO BET.
>
> *Damon Runyon*

NEW BEGINNINGS

In the beginning there was the physician. Then came the hospital. And for more than a century they combined their best efforts and resources to care for the sick.

Today that comfortable relationship has been upset and industry guesstimators make a strong case for its never again reappearing in its old form.

Today, physicians and hospitals find themselves vulnerable to each other's resources, competitors for patients, and assaulted by a variety of forces economically.

What's the solution?

The brightest, more practical physicians and hospitals are responding to the crisis not with temporary Band-Aid measures but with new, strong business alliances that can ensure them both a place in the new health care sun that is shining so thinly over the landscape.

These alliances, as noted throughout, are called joint ventures. The very phrase joint ventures has strong connotations and implications.

- Joint means together in an equal sense.
- Joint means to achieve the same goal or end result.
- Venture implies a corporate or business structure and relationship.
- Joint means to share in the risks as well as the rewards.
- Venture implies capital and a bottom line.
- Joint venture has sense of togetherness, not aloneness, in what is rapidly becoming a hostile operating environment.

For both to survive, physicians and hospitals must work together, share together, and risk together for any kind of reward.

However, there are guidelines and checklists that must be taken into account for both partners to achieve satisfaction and survival. This section outlines areas critical to the success of physician-hospital joint ventures.

List in order of importance to your facility the reasons for economic cooperation with physicians

_____ Prospective payment systems
_____ Health maintenance organizations
_____ Ambulatory surgical care centers
_____ Peer review organizations
_____ Relative value scales
_____ State regulation of physician fees
_____ Competition between individual physicians and physician groups

NEW ALTERNATIVES IN WORKING WITH PHYSICIANS

Alternative # 1: MeSH

Definition

A MeSH Plan is a medical (Me) staff (S) hospital (H) joint venture.

Benefits of a MeSH

- explore new business
- determine markets for new products and services
- feed products and services into new markets

Considerations in Forming a MeSH

- When should you present the concept to the medical staff?
- How many members of the medical staff should be invited to join?
- How will the MeSH develop new delivery systems?
- What kind of a workable and manageable structure will be organized?

Questions To Ask Yourself in Forming a MeSH

1. Who will be on the original committee to develop the concept?
   a. ______________________________
   b. ______________________________
   c. ______________________________
   d. ______________________________
2. Who will act as legal counsel? ______________________________
   Alternative choice: ______________________________
3. What will be the organizational/corporate structure:
   a. Not for profit
      Benefits: 1. ______________________________
      2. ______________________________
      3. ______________________________
      Negatives: 1. ______________________________
      2. ______________________________
      3. ______________________________
   b. Taxable corporation
      Benefits: 1. ______________________________
      2. ______________________________
      3. ______________________________

Negatives: 1. ______________________
2. ______________________
3. ______________________

4. What are the rights of the hospital and physicians to withdraw?
   a. ______________________
   b. ______________________
   c. ______________________
5. What is the statement of purpose?
   ____
   ____
   ____
6. What are the key elements to be contained in the bylaws?
   a. ______________________
   b. ______________________
   c. ______________________
7. What is the product mix of the MeSH?
   a. ______________________
   b. ______________________
   c. ______________________
8. What are the areas in which the MeSH has no rights vis-à-vis its members?
   a. ______________________
   b. ______________________
   c. ______________________

Alternative # 2: HEPP

Definition

A HEPP is a Hospital Economic Profile Policy. It is a program whereby physicians are given incentives to be alert to the financial implementations that their treatment decisions will have for their hospital.

Benefits of a HEPP

- Cash compensation
- Deferred compensation plans for physicians
- Educational programs or mandatory consultation for identified physicians
- Contractual commitments
- Requirements imposed by new medical staff bylaws provisions, including the potential for restrictions on privileges.

Considerations in Forming an HEPP

- When should you present this concept to the medical staff?
- How will the HEPP relate to the new delivery systems?
- How will the HEPP program be structured?

Questions To Ask Yourself in Forming an HEPP

1. Who will be on the commitee to develop and help present the concept to physicians?
   a. ______________________________
   b. ______________________________
   c. ______________________________
   d. ______________________________
2. Who will administer the operation of the HEPP? __________
   Alternate choice
   ____
3. What will be the organizational/corporate structure of the program?
   a. Hospital administered? If so, how? __________
      ____
      ____
   b. Physician administered? If so, how? __________
      ____
   c. Joint hospital-physician administered? If so, how? __________
      ____
      ____
4. What are the rights of the hospital and physicians to withdraw or cancel the plan?
   a. ______________________________
   b. ______________________________
   c. ______________________________
5. What is the statement of purpose?
   ____
   ____
6. How will the types of incentives be determined and allocated, and by whom?
   ____
   ____
7. What will the physician education and consultation programs consist of, how can physicians be required to attend, and who will do the "teaching" or consulting?
   a. Program content: __________
   ____

b. Attendance: ____

____

c. Educator-consultants: ______________________________

8. What will the contractual commitments require each party to do?
   a. ____
   b. ____
   c. ____
9. How will the program requirements relate to medical staff bylaws, particularly on restrictions on privileges?

   ____

   ____

WRAP-UP

There are dozens of different products, markets, and mixes to consider when forming a joint venture with physicians just as there are dozens of different organizational forms that might make the best fit. It is important to take time and talk with your prospective joint partners and hammer out a feasible, workable project together from the very start.

There is no question that the "times they are a-changin'." With a lot of trust, cooperation, and planning, they may even be changing for the better.

HOSPITALS WITH VENTURE CAPITALISTS

> THE FIRST LAW OF ECONOMICS
>
> THERE IS NO SUCH THING AS A FREE LUNCH.
>
> *Burton Crane*

> LEONTIEF'S PARADOX
>
> IN THE UNITED STATES, CAPITAL RATHER THAN LABOR IS THE RELATIVELY SCARCE FACTOR OF PRODUCTION.
>
> *Leontief*

HIGHLIGHTS

- Finding the Dollars
- Benefits
- Do Your Homework
- Important Warnings

WHERE THE DOLLARS ARE . . . THERE ARE THE VENTURE CAPITALISTS

The health care industry in the mid-1980s report economic activity in the $300 billion range and employed more than six million persons. Numbers like that make the financial community sit up and take notice.

Furthermore the industry itself is in a state of flux. New ventures are forming, new business opportunities are being explored, and new markets are being discovered daily.

Add to this mix the spiralling cost of high-technology diagnostic equipment, the capital needed to fund research and development, and the potential for huge profits and you have the perfect, financially fertile field for forming a joint venture with a venture capital company.

However, as with all prospective partners, there are certain things to be aware of—more so in dealing with venture capitalists than perhaps with any other group.

WHERE TO FIND VENTURE CAPITALISTS

There are really only a few solid sources for finding a venture capitalist and these are by referral only:

- Your bank
- Your law firm
- Your accounting firm

PLUSES WITH VENTURE CAPITALISTS

- If a venture capitalist "bites" (agrees to finance you), you can be sure that the project is valid and has a high probability of being successful and generating a profit. Venture capitalists are in the business of making money.

- Venture capitalists bring a great deal of business acumen and management expertise into the venture with them, two comodities that health care partners often sadly lack.
- Venture capitalists will take the larger financial burden, allowing the hospital to do what it does well—help patients.

BEFORE YOU APPROACH A VENTURE CAPITAL FIRM

1. Develop a solid business plan.
2. Do extensive market surveys.
3. Line up your own experts in finance, law, accounting.
4. Understand the ethical implications of the project.
5. Get agreement from your side that the venture capital route is the best one to take for your particular venture.

RED FLAGS

- Venture capitalists have a different mission in many cases from the players on the health care side. The venture capital team is interested in making money. This is a critical consideration for any hospital administrator to consider before hopping into bed with them.
- Venture capitalists, by providing the capital, often request and receive the lion's share of the venture. This means the hospital runs the risk of abdicating control of the venture to the lender, particularly in its critical formative stages.
- Venture capitalists make tough deals. These are the big-money boys and they have a lot more experience in evaluating and managing projects than do the health care partners. Venture capitalists play a dominant management role in the project and their management style may not be acceptable to the hospital.

HOSPITALS WITH OTHER COMPANIES

> ONE OF THE STRONGEST ALLIES IN AMERICA'S HEALTH HABIT TRANSFORMATION IS THE BUSINESS COMMUNITY . . .
>
> *John Naisbitt*

HIGHLIGHTS

- Unlikely Allies
- From a Business Point of View
- From a Health Care Point of View
- Finding the Right Business Partner

BUSINESS AND MEDICINE: UNLIKELY ALLIES

At first shock it seems like an unlikely union—hard-nosed business and health care. But upon closer examination the link makes sense.

From a Business Point of View

1. Business wants healthy employees—sick ones cost money.
2. Business is increasingly concerned about the spiraling costs of health insurance.
3. Business is looking for new markets for its own products and the health care industry is being perceived as a potential area for doing business.

From a Health Care Point of View

1. Hospitals are looking for markets and products for their own increasingly competitive situation.
2. Hospitals can rent out their unused space and create income.
3. Hospitals, by joint venturing with other businesses, can generate nontraditional profit centers for themselves.

POTENTIAL GOOD BUSINESS PARTNERS

Pharmaceutical Companies

List pharmaceutical companies with which you have established good relationships

____

____

____

Other Suppliers

One of the best partners to develop is one with which you already do business. List all hospital suppliers that might be approached:

____

____

____

Businesses Thriving in the Community

Drive through your local area and make a list of businesses that might make good partners:

a. Food Chains/Restaurants

____

____

____

b. Hotels

____

____

---

c. Related Medical Services: Optometrists, etc.

---

d. Fitness Institutes/Diet Centers

---

e. Video Suppliers

Appendix A*

Alternative Legal Models for Joint Ventures

SUBCHAPTER T COOPERATIVE

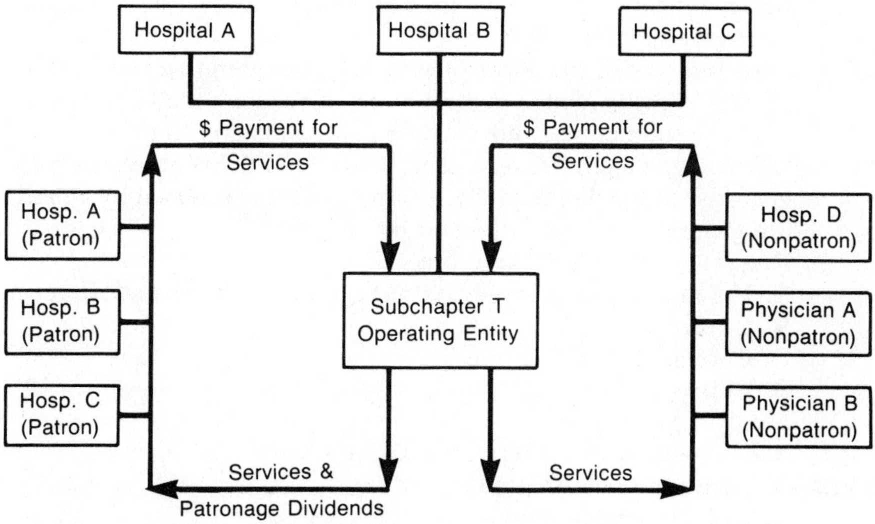

Figure A-1 Diagram of a Subchapter T Venture

*Appendixes A–G are adapted with permission from material contributed by Gary W. Eiland of the law firm of Wood, Lucksinger & Epstein, Houston.

Also, please note that a "Key to Alphabet Soup" for Appendixes A–G follows Appendix G.

DEFINITION AND DESCRIPTION

I. A corporation may make a subchapter T election (see Figure A-1) if it is organized on a cooperative basis

II. The cooperative must be democratically controlled by individuals designated as patrons. The cooperative determines who will be designated as a patron, but at least 50 percent of its business must be with patrons. Generally, the hospital and CSPs are designated as patrons.

III. Dividends paid to patrons, called patronage dividends, are deductible for federal tax purposes by the cooperative as a business expense. The term "patronage dividend" is defined as an amount paid to a patron by a cooperative organization that satisfies the following conditions:
   A. The amount is determined by reference to the net earnings of the cooperative organization from business done with or for its patrons and is paid on the basis of the quantity or value of the business done with or for the patron, and
   B. There is a valid, enforceable, and preexisting written obligation to pay such amounts

IV. Distributions in the form of patronage dividends to each patron must be directly related to the volume of business each patron refers to the venture entity, and must be made pursuant to the terms of a written agreement between each patron and the venture entity that gives rise to the dividend. Patronage dividends received by a patron are generally subject to federal income tax.

V. Reimbursement considerations:
   A. Fraud and abuse implications regarding rebates and discounts
   B. Coverage and certification
   C. Capital cost pass-through
   D. Billing

VI. Medical practice act.

VII. State commercial bribery/antikickback laws.

VIII. Application of securities laws.
   A. Stock of corporation
   B. Patron interest

XIV. Tax considerations
   A. ITC pass-through
   B. Risk of retroactive denial of subchapter T status

Appendix B

Coordination of Structure and Operational Issues

CHOICE OF JOINT VENTURE ENTITY FORMAT

I. Multiple legal forms for the entity are available
   A. Primary alternatives:
      1. Corporation (C, S, or T)
      2. General partnership
      3. Limited partnership

II. Considerations in selection structure

III. Elements of structure (assuming use of a corporation)
   A. Two common classes of shares, with one shareholder in each class:
      1. Individualized hospital and other participants' shareholder powers (e.g. select/remove their respective appointed directors)
      2. Joint hospital and other shareholder powers
         a) General, e.g.:
            (1) approve change in entity (articles, merger, consolidation, liquidation)
            (2) approve sale of substantially all assets (go out of business)
         b) Specially reserved (few required because of composition of board), e.g.:
            (1) approve sale of securities
            (2) approve annual capital/operating budgets
            (3) approve unbudgeted purchases, commitments in excess of preset amount
            (4) approve duality transactions with hospital or other participants
            (5) approve bylaw changes

(6) cause liquidation (N.B.: different presumptions between general partnership and corporation)

3. Meetings and actions
   a) Provide for meetings
   b) Plan on action by written consent of board

B. Board:
   1. Membership (10 to 13)
      a) Appointed by two respective shareholders
         (1) five hospital representatives
         (2) five other participant representatives
      b) Option for three directors to be elected by board
         (1) venture president
         (2) two from outside
      c) Option for nonvoting consulting director(s) (e.g., counsel)
   2. Five-five board deadlocks, how avoided or broken
      a) Outsiders may mitigate against creation of a psychological deadlock
      b) Final authority reservation techniques
         (1) reserve to shareholders
         (2) require majority of each director class
   3. Powers
      a) General business and affairs
      b) Select officers
   4. Manner of acting
      a) Regular and special meeting
         (1) monthly to start
         (2) quarterly thereafter
      b) Notice and waiver
      c) Quorum
         (1) present at site or by telephone
         (2) by proxy
      d) Action
         (1) at meeting by majority vote (which majority must include a majority of both hospital and CSP directors except with respect to the enforcement of central rights vis-à-vis hospital or CSP shareholder entities)
         (2) by unanimous written consent
   5. Reimbursement/compensation
      a) Reimbursement, for all
      b) Compensation, perhaps nominal director fees for outsiders if used

- C. Officers (employed professional versus volunteers):
  - 1. President
  - 2. Vice president, treasurer, and secretary
- D. Committees:
  - 1. Board committees (committees with power to exercise all or a portion of the powers of board between meetings of board may not be required)
    - *a*) Nature (of board by board)
    - *b*) Possible committee functions
      - (1) executive
      - (2) appeals
      - (3) audit
  - 2. Corporate committees
    - *a*) Nature (advisory to board by president with board approval)
    - *b*) Possible
      - (1) system planning
      - (2) new venture feasibility
      - (3) existing venture administration
      - (4) services
  - 3. Administrative committees
    - *a*) Nature (advisory to president by president)
    - *b*) Possible
- E. Indemnification and insurance

IV. Ownership and control of venture

- A. Premise re venture
  - 1. Two primary venturers, equality
  - 2. Technique
    - *a*) Equal equity ownership
    - *b*) Equal equity control
  - 3. Not the only way
  - 4. If not equality of control, venture moves closer to either classic:
    - *a*) Physician-controlled hospital or
    - *b*) Hospital-controlled physician
- B. Capital financing of venture
  - 1. Quantum
  - 2. Method
    - *a*) Common equity securities
    - *b*) Preferred equity securities
    - *c*) Variety of debt securities

C. Operating financing
  1. Sale of services
    a) Hospital
    b) Ventures
    c) Others
  2. Earnings from ventures
D. Capital and operating financing and control of ventures
  1. Capital and operating financing
    a) Capital
      (1) venture entity
      (2) others
    b) Control

V. Governance of joint venture
  A. Governance vehicles
    1. Shareholder governance
    2. Board governance
    3. Executive governance
  B. Balanced/unbalanced
  C. Functions of board
    1. Establishment of strategic plan (including identification and evaluation of venture opportunities) and periodic review and revision of that plan
    2. Selection of senior management team
    3. Review and approval of initial business plans for all new ventures, including type of business, operational management team, financing arrangements, marketing strategies, risk and incentive programs for providers, etc.
    4. Appointment of governing body members for all ventures
    5. Periodic review of operating performance of all ventures and consolidated system operations
    6. Serving as a review board to evaluate internal disputes or grievances arising between system members and ventures
  D. Frequency of meetings
  E. Mechanics of meetings

VI. Functions of staff of joint venture
  A. Strategic planning to define broad strategy that will result in joint venture system's acting to benefit both basic partners
  B. Identification of specific venture opportunities consistent with mission
  C. Development and implementation of ventures that have been approved
  D. Provision of general management supervision and support for existing ventures

E. Operation of central support services required by the various ventures, including financial management, design and operation of information systems, operation of PR, and marketing services.

JOINT VENTURE PARTICIPANTS

I. Can be any type of legal entity
II. Membership in the case of physician entities can be limited to physicians:
    A. Active on medical staff
    B. Individual election to join joint venture
    C. Staff privileges not dependent upon decision to join
III. Participants' organization considerations
    A. Covenants (e.g., right of first refusal)
    B. Capital investment
        1. Quantum/division/time
            a) Quantum $500–$1,500
            b) Division
                (1) stock fixed price
                (2) initiation
            c) Year one eligibility and subsequently
        2. Restrictions
    C. Annual dues
    D. Prerogatives:
        1. Voting on decisions
        2. First participation opportunity
        3. Income
    E. No restriction on:
        1. Private practice
        2. Medical staff rights
        3. Other plans

Appendix C

Securities

I. A security: any note, stock, bond, or participation in any profit-sharing arrangement, including subscriptions or preorganization funding

II. Applicability of securities laws to joint ventures

  A. Securities laws are applicable to the offering of interests in jointly owned entity

    1. Possible exception is joint venture involving limited number of parties in which all will participate actively in its operation

    2. A transaction should be examined to determine if it involves the person's investing dollars:

      a) In a common enterprise

      b) expecting profits

      c) expecting those profits through efforts of a promoter or third party

  B. Sale of stock or limited partnership interest requires compliance with antifraud statutes and may require compliance with the registration requirements of federal and state securities laws unless exemption requirements are met

  C. Registration may be a plus because it adds credibility and flexibility; costs may be controlled

III. Available federal registration exemptions

  A. Most frequently used is intrastate offering exemption, which is available if:

    1. Issuer of securities is a resident of a single state (state of incorporation or organization if a corporation or limited partnership, and if principal office is a general partnership)

    2. Issuer derives at least 80 percent of its consolidated gross revenues from that state, has at least 80 percent of its consolidated assets in that state, intends to use at least 80 percent

of offering proceeds in that state, and has its principal office located in that state

3. All offers and sales are made to persons who are residents of that state (have principal office within the state if a corporation, partnership, trust, or other form of business organization)
4. Resale of shares or interests is prohibited to any person not a resident of such state for nine months from date of last sale made in offering

B. If sales are made across state lines, private placement exemption under Reg. D of the Securities Act of 1933 will be available if:
   1. No general solicitation or advertisement is used in selling the securities
   2. Resale of securities is limited to compliance with federal and state securities law (severe limitations on resale)
   3. Sales are made to no more than 35 nonaccredited investors (see definition below) and to an unlimited number of accredited investors.
   4. Specific information is disseminated to all purchasers in form of an Offering Memorandum, unless all investors are accredited investors; if all purchasers are accredited investors, information still must be furnished sufficient to protect issuer from fraud claims
   5. Type of information to be furnished and number of persons to whom sales can be made to vary, depending on amount of dollars being raised, the significant dollar amounts being:
      a) Less than $500,000
      b) Less than $5 million
      c) More than $5 million
   6. Form D must be filed with the SEC promptly after the first sale

C. Definition of accredited investor
   1. If an entity: A bank, insurance company, registered investment company, private business development company, or tax-exempt organization with total assets in excess of $5 million
   2. If an employee benefit plan: One with total assets in excess of $5 million or one in which investment decision is made by a plan fiduciary that is either a bank, insurance company, or registered investment adviser
   3. If an individual, either:
      a) An executive officer or director of the issuer
      b) One whose individual net worth or joint net worth with spouse at the time of purchase exceeds $1 million

c) One who had individual income in excess of $200,000 in each of two most recent years and who reasonably expects income in excess of $200,000 in current year

d) One who purchases at least $150,000 of securities where total purchase price (cash and notes) does not exceed 20 percent of the individual's net worth at time of the sale, or joint net worth with spouse

4. Any entity in which all equity owners are accredited investors under any of above categories
5. Certain related persons, corporations, partnerships, trusts, or other controlled entities may not be counted twice
6. Physicians as a class are not assumed to be accredited investors

IV. If intrastate exception is available, state registration exemptions may be available

V. In addition to one of the above federal exemptions, sales of securities must qualify under limited offering exemption of applicable state securities laws; e.g., applicable provisions of the Texas Securities Act, which are somewhat typical of most states, are:

A. Sales may be made to no more than 35 nonaccredited investors (and an unlimited number of accredited investors) within last 12 months by that issuer (by contrast, Pennsylvania restricts *offering* to no more than 10 nonaccredited investors)

B. Neither issuer nor any of its executive officers or directors may have been charged with or convicted of certain securities violations

C. No public solicitation or advertisement may be used in the sale of securities

D. Each investor must either

1. have a prior relationship with issuer evidencing trust
2. be an accredited investor or
3. have financial net worth at least five times the size of investor's investment and be knowledgeable and experienced in finance, securities, and investments generally (or have a purchaser representative who provides such knowledge and experience)

E. Specific written information about offering must be provided to investors in form of an Offering Memorandum

F. Securities must be purchased for investment only without a view to distribution and must be restricted in their resale

G. Notice must be filed with the Texas Securities Commission 10 days before any sale can be made in the state (may be avoided, depending on presence of a registered dealer, number of purchasers, number of security holders, and number of accredited investors)

VI. No exemption from the antifraud statutes of the federal or state securities laws

VII. Typical offering memorandum would include the following sections:
   A. Important Notices
   B. The Company
   C. Risk Factors
   D. Dividend Policy
   E. The Offering
   F. Use of Proceeds
   G. Management
   H. Principal Stockholders
   I. Description of Capital Stock
   J. Determination of Offering Price.

Appendix D

Criminal Statutes

I. Federal law

  A. Medicare/Medicaid fraud and abuse provisions

    1. Definitions

      a) Fraud: Knowing and willful deception or misrepresentation—or a reckless disregard of the facts—with intent to receive an unauthorized benefit

      b) Abuse: Incidents and practices that, although not considered fraudulent acts, may directly or indirectly cause financial losses to the Medicare program or to beneficiaries and their families, HIM-13, § 3454 (anything the agent dislikes but for which he is unable to obtain an indictment)

    2. Areas of potential violation

      a) Knowing, willful, and repeated violations of assignment—42 U.S.C. § 1395nn(d) (Medicare only)

      b) Material misrepresentations (Medicare/Medicaid False Claims Act)—42 U.S.C. § 1395nn(a); 1396h(a):

        (1) statutory proscriptions

          (*a*) false statements or misrepresentation in benefit or payment application process

          (*b*) false statements or misrepresentation in benefit or payment adjudication process

          (*c*) failure to disclose subsequent event affecting initial or continuing right to retain benefit or payment

          (*d*) conversion of benefit or payment received on behalf of another

        (2) penalty (felony, 5 years, $25,000)

c) Illegal remuneration—42 U.S.C. § 1395nn(b) Medicare), 42 U.S.C. § 1369h(b) (Medicaid)

(1) penalty (felony, 5 years, $25,000)

(2) flow of "value" from provider/supplier to referral source

(*a*) contractual relationships

(i) payment for referral or patient service opportunities

Example: Part A/B I.L. No. 83-19/83-11, Dec. 1983 (MEDICARE & MEDICAID GUIDE CCH ¶ 33,553) Manufacturers offering pacemaker monitoring equipment to hospitals and physicians at no charge to induce purchase of their model pacemakers and manufacturers of intraocular lenses furnishing additional products or gifts to ophthalmologists in exchange for ordering their products warned of possible violation of § 1877(b) of Social Security Act; and

Example: *United States v. Ruttenberg,* 625 F.2d 173 (7th Cir. 1980). Court upheld conviction of druggist who paid monthly fees to nursing home owners for the opportunity of providing drugs and other items to Medicaid recipients in the homes

(ii) payment for nonperformed consulting services

Example: *United States v. Greber,* 760 F.2d 68 (1985). Company providing diagnostic services such as Holter monitoring paid physicians "interpretation fees" for each patient even though company itself actually evaluated the monitor service. To the extent that payments to the physicians were made to induce them to refer their Medicare patients to use company's services, Medicare fraud was established, even if the payments also were intended to compensate for professional services

(iii) referral condition of contract; opportunity/contract covers only referred patients

Example: Part B I.L. No. 85-2, April 1985 (supersedes 84-9) MEDICARE & MEDICAID GUIDE (CCH)

¶ 34,544) Durable medical equipment (DME) suppliers paying "finder" or referral fees to respiratory therapists may be in violation of 42 U.S.C. § 1395nn, 1396h; therefore, carriers instructed to so inform these suppliers and report any activities of this type to Inspector General (IG)

(iv) Contract payments computed on number of referred patients

Example: *United States v. Hancock,* 604 F.2d 999 (7th Cir. 1979). Chiropractors claimed payments from a laboratory were handling fees, but court construed as kickbacks.

(*b*) investment relationships

(i) referrals as condition of investment opportunity

(ii) below-market investment opportunity

Example: *Unived States v. Universal Trade and Industry,* 695 F.2d 1151 (9th Cir. 1983). An onsite laboratory was set up at a medical clinic, with stock in laboratory given to clinic without any equity contribution. Court held that provision of laboratory at no cost to medical clinic and payments to clinic's physicians based on percentage of gross laboratory revenues constituted a "kickback scheme" that violated illegal remuneration statute. Court noted that physicians provided no administrative or other services in exchange for payments, and, that payments were directly related to number of tests referred by clinic to laboratory

(iii) distributions contingent on referrals or based on profits from referred patients

(iv) buyout if fail to refer (negative incentive)

(3) exclusions

(*a*) discounts obtained: law specifically excludes practice of discounting or other reductions in price from range of financial transactions to be considered illegal under Medicare and Medicaid, *but only* if such discounts are properly disclosed and reflected in costs for which reimbursement could be claimed

(*b*) bona fide employment relationships

(*c*) complaint sources:
(i) excluded physician investors
(ii) disgruntled former investors/employees/contractors

B. Other Federal Statutes
1. The Travel Act, 18 U.S.C.A. 1952, was designed to eradicate organized crime with an interstate nexus. It has been applied in federal prosecutions against defendants who violated state commercial bribery statutes. *United States v. Perrin,* 580 F.2d 730 (5th Cir. 1978)
2. Racketeer Influenced and Corrupt Organizations Act (RICO), 18 U.S.C.A. § § 1961–1968, represents an effort to quell the influence of organized crime in legitimate enterprises. RICO also could be used against a defendant who violates state bribery laws

II. State Law
A. Commercial bribery statutes generally prohibit a fiduciary acting without the consent of the beneficiary from intentionally or knowingly soliciting, accepting, or agreeing to accept any benefit from another person to influence the fiduciary's conduct toward the beneficiary. (TEX. PENAL CODE ANN. § 32.43; LA. REV. STAT. ANN. § 14.73; ILL. ANN. STAT. ch. 38 § 29A (Smith-Hurd 1982–1983)
1. "Fiduciary" includes an agent or employee; a trustee, guardian, custodian, receiver; a lawyer, physician, accountant; or an officer, director, partner or manager of a corporation or association. (TEX. PENAL CODE ANN. § 32.43).

B. State medical practice acts often provide criminal sanctions against physicians who pay other persons for referrals or who receive payments from other physicians for referrals

III. AMA Ethical Standards
A. Physician must disclose financial interest in any project to which patient is referred

Appendix E

Antitrust Considerations

I. Definition and Objectives
   A. Antitrust is business conduct or practice that unreasonably restrains or limits the competitive forces in the market
   B. Antitrust objectives are:
      1. To reduce the cost of providing goods and services and to improve the quantity and quality of consumer alternatives
      2. To produce lower prices and better goods and services through competition
   C. Antitrust law is based on statutes but explained through case law
      1. Analysis in many cases depends on the facts, although per se violations are not dependent on facts
      2. The health care industry traditionally considered itself immune, but beginning in 1975, cases have narrowed the scope of immunity, if any
         a) *Goldfarb v. Virginia State Bar/Ass'n* 95 S. Ct. 2004 (1975). U.S. Supreme Court held that bar association fee schedules are not exempt from antitrust; Struck down "learned profession" exception that in past had protected health care field
         b) *Hospital Building Co. v. Trustees of Rex Hosp.,* 96 S. Ct. 1848 (1976). Hospitals (and probably clinics) are part of interstate commerce. Struck down old doctrine that health care was not covered by federal statutes
         c) *Arizona v. Maricopa County Medical Soc'y,* 102 S. Ct. 2466 (1982). Health care institutions can be liable for price fixing as a per se violation of antitrust laws; court struck down argument that health care should be treated under rule of

reason; important indication that general business standards will be applied to field

d) *American Soc'y of Medical Eng'rs v. Hydro Level Corp.,* 102 S. Ct. 1935 (1982). Nonprofit organization may be held civilly liable under antitrust statutes

II. Sherman Act

A. Section I of Sherman Act prohibits contracts, combinations, or conspiracies in restrain of trade

1. General applicability: Unlawful agreements prohibited among competitors whether they concern buying or selling activities of competitors (horizontal agreements) or they are among elements of a distribution chain for products or services (vertical agreements)

2. Restraints of trade

a) Rule of Reason: Whether a practice is unlawful under Section I is judged by all the circumstances, including potential procompetitive effects of the particular restraint

(1) *National Soc'y of Professional Eng'rs v. United States,* 435 U.S. 679 (1979). Reasonableness of individual purchaser's decision not to seek lower prices through competition does not authorize vendors to conspire to impose that same decision on all other purchasers

(2) requirement by PPO that providers deal exclusively with that PPO and no others. *The Wall Street Journal,* Oct. 15, 1984, article on Modesto, Cal., PPO closing in face of opposition by Justice Department

b) Per Se Restraint: Some practices are recognized by courts as so plainly anticompetitive that they are considered violations of Section I without consideration of any other factors of analysis

(1) price fixing: direct setting of prices by competitors, which includes effect of stabilizing prices or suppressing competition in pricing, such as common price discounts or exchanging price information, is prohibited. *Arizona v. Maricopa County Medical Soc'y,* 457 U.S. 332 (1982). A relative value scale (RVS) published by a medical association could have anticompetition effects. F.T.C. Advisory Opinion, *Amer. Society of Internal Medicine,* File NO. P843532

(2) refusal to deal: this is the group boycott, agreement among competitors to refrain from doing business with others and as such per se violation. *Virginia Academy of*

Clinical Psychologists v. Blue Shield of Virginia, 624 F.2d 476 (4th Cir. 1980). This includes situations where one group of competitors, because of its market power, controls facilities needed by other competitors and refuses to allow them access. Thus, membership rules must be fair and no more restrictive than necessary to serve legitimate competitive group needs. *Marrese v. American Academy of Orthopedic Surgeons,* 706 F.2d 1488–1495 (7th Cir. 1983). *Realty Multilist,* 629 F.2d, 1351 (5th Cir. 1980)

(3) market allocation: agreements among competitors to divide the market either geographically by type of service or product or type of customer are per se violations. In *Robinson v. McGovern,* 521 F. Supp. 842 (1981), a Pennsylvania case regarding cardiovascular surgeon, relevant geographic market was held to be territory within which defendant could operate without encountering other suppliers who have right to compete on substantial parity. Relevant product market consists of "products that have reasonable interchangeability for the purposes for which they are produced—prices, use, and quantities considered." *U.S. v. E.I. duPont de Nemours and Co.,* 351 U.S. 377, 404 (1956)

(4) tying arrangements: arrangement in which sellers with substantial market power sell one product only on condition that another product be purchased at same time. "Analysis must consider whether two separate products that may be tied together are being sold, and if so, whether petitioners have used their market power to force their patients to accept the tying arrangement." *Jefferson Parish Hosp. Dist. No. 2 v. Hyde,* 104 S. Ct. 1551 (1985)

c) If a group of competitors combine and form a new and separate entity with new productive capacity or a new product, result could promote competition. Restraints within such a group, even if they relate to prices, may not violate Section I because only one entity is involved. *Arizona v. Maricopa County Medical Soc'y,* 457 U.S. 332 (1982). See also *Broadcast Music, Inc. v. Columbia Broadcasting Systm,* 441 U.S. 1 (1979) and *Ratino v. Medical Serv. of District of Columbia,* 718 F.2d 1260 (1983).

d) "The practical difference between a per se offense and a rule of reason offense is that under the per se rule, anticompetitive impact of the alleged offense is presumed while under the rule of reason its anticompetitive impact must be proven." *Hospital Building Co. v. Trustees of Rex Hos.,* 691 F.2d 678, 684 (4th Cir. 1982), *reh'g denied,* 104 S. Ct. 512 (1984).

B. Section II of the Sherman Act prohibits any attempt to monopolize the market
   1. Mere size is not enough, it is the power to exclude that is the key; there are two elements in this offense: (1) the possession of monopoly power and (2) the willful acquisition or maintenance of that power as distinguished from growth or development as a consequence of superior product, business acumen, or historic accident; unless it is economically inevitable, it is generally a violation of Section II for any entity having effective control over the market to use or plan to use any exclusionary practice
      a) Legitimate business reasons for refusal to discontinue "all-mountains" package ski tickets do not violate law, even if defendant is found to possess monopoly power; concern is with conduct that unnecessarily excludes or handicaps competitors. *Aspen Skiing Co. v. Aspen Highland Skiing Corp.,* 105 S. Ct. 2847 (1985)
   2. Market power
      a) Definition relevant to market
         (1) geographic market
         (2) degree of market power
            (*a*) "Twenty (20) percent or more of the market creates substantial risk of scrutiny under Section II; less is usually not scrutinized. In fact, some providers must be left out if preferred provider organizations are to succeed." (Remarks of Paul McGrath, Assistant Attorney General, Antitrust Division, Third Annual ABA Antitrust Spring Meeting, March 22, 1985)
            (*b*) joint ventures may avoid violations of Section I because they are legitimate business endeavors, only to violate Section II because they control too much of the relevant market. *See* circumstances regarding Modesto, Cal., proposed PPO, *The Wall Street Journal,* Oct. 15, 1984

C. Exemptions and defenses
   1. State action exemption: a state, in exercising its sovereign power, enacts legislation opposing certain anticompetitive restraints where Sherman Act won't apply. *Parker v. Brown,* 317 U.S. 341 (1943)
   2. Health planning: *National Gerimedical and Gerontology Center v. Blue Cross of Kansas,* 452 U.S. 378 (1981). Voluntary actions taken under health planning statutes do not automatically confer antitrust immunity. Instead, they must be defended under rule-of-reason analysis. *Hospital Building Co. v. Trustees of Rex Hosp.,* 691 F.2d 678, 685 (4th Cir. 1982), *reh'g denied,* 104 U.S. 512 (1983)

III. Robinson Patman Act
   A. This act provides that discrimination in price, services, or facilities is illegal but nonprofit institutions are exempt from price discrimination provisions
   B. Independent pharmacists' action against an insurance company and three pharmacies for allegedly entering agreements to fix retail drug and pharmaceutical prices resulted in court's finding agreements were not the "business of insurance" so as to fall under the McCarran-Ferguson Act exemption from antitrust laws. *Group Life and Health Ins. Co. v. Royal Drug Co.,* 99 S. Ct. 1067, cert. denied, 105 S. Ct. 912 (1985).
   C. This creates a problem for joint ventures such as home health agencies with nonprofit hospital and for-profit subsidiary that is given an improper advantage via pass-through of tax-exempt business's "taxbreak."

IV. Clayton Act
   A. This act makes it unlawful for a sale or contract to be premised under agreement not to use competitor's goods or services when effect is to substantially lessen competition or to create a monopoly
   B. Exclusive contract issues have arisen on numerous occasions under Clayton Act. Courts have almost uniformly upheld contracts between hospitals and physicians providing for exclusive medical services
      1. Exclusive anesthesia contract upheld, *Jefferson Parish Hosp. Dist. No. 2 v. Hyde,* 104 S. Ct., 1551 (1984). Exclusive contracts generally have been evaluated under rule-of-reason approach. However, decision in *Hyde* clearly indicates that exclusive con-

tracts may not be valid where provider's agreement leaves consumers with no reasonable choice

2. Exclusive emergency room contract upheld, *Smith v. Northern Michigan Hospitals, Inc.,* 703 F.2d 942 (6th Cir. 1983)
3. Exclusive contract between hospital and radiologists upheld as reasonable exercise of power to provide proper hospital management. *Williams v. Hobbs,* 460 N.E.2d 287 (1983)

V. Federal Trade Commission Act
   A. This act provides that unfair methods of competition and unfair or deceptive acts or practices are illegal when they are in or affecting commerce
   B. Technically, FTC actions apply only to for-profit corporations but this mandate has been broadly interpreted.
   C. Factors encouraging FTC entry into health care industry:
      1. Increased consumer activity
      2. Recent U.S. Supreme Court decisions extending federal antitrust authority to professional activities and associations
      3. Economic character of health care industry, which represents almost 10 percent of the gross national product, more than $212 billion in 1980
   C. *Health Care Management Associates,* 101 F.T.C. 1014 (1983), and *California Medical Association,* F.T.C. Docket No. C-2967 (1985) reflect current FTC opinions on PPOs and RVS development, as do *The Wall Street Journal,* Oct. 15, 1984, article on the proposed Modesto, Cal., PPO and F.T.C. Advisory Opinion, *Amer. Society of Internal Medicine,* File No. P84353

VI. State Antitrust Statutes
   A. These are systems by which states regulate trade practices; "Little Sherman Acts" enacted by most states have a substantial impact on regulation of intrastate commerce; most of these statutes closely follow Sherman Act itself and often may not be used substantially because of their similarity to federal statute
   B. Various state statutes, however, differently define entities in the health care arena that may or may not be covered by state antitrust statutes; for example:
      1. Washington defines prepaid plans as products
      2. California does not apply its antitrust statutes to practice of medicine because it is a profession, but in Florida medicine is defined as a business
   C. State consumer protection acts also prohibit unfair competition and deceptive or unconscionable acts or practices, and often are used in conjunction with various trade practice statutes

VII. Antitrust Impact on Joint Venture Entities

A. A joint venture entity may be characterized as a partial vertical integration involving various links in the health care chain and as such does not propose antitrust problems unless a single joint venture entity has a dominant market share in a given market.

B. Potential antitrust problems could arise if a joint venture were to:

1. Fix prices in an effort to control the market by stabilizing prices or suppressing competitors' pricing
2. Restrict membership to a single joint venture entity
3. Enforce a right of first refusal
4. Include a covenant not to compete

C. Individual ventures may raise various antitrust issues that should be addressed at the planning stage.

Appendix F

Medical Practice Considerations

MEDICAL PRACTICE

I. Corporate practice of medicine prohibition

A. General purpose: To prevent a licensed physician from being controlled by a corporation or unlicensed individual in diagnosis and treatment of patients. It has been codified in only about 17 states, and varies in extent and strength of enforcement from state to state

B. Distinguish from issue of whether physicians can incorporate their practice of medicine

1. Some states allow professional corporations for the practice of medicine where they are organized solely and specifically for rendering professional services and have as their shareholders only individuals authorized to render the same professional services as corporation; other states' statutes specifically exclude physicians from professional corporations

C. Essence of prohibition where applied

1. State statutes

a) Texas Medical Practice Act, TEX. REV. CIV. STAT. ANN. art. 4495b (Vernon 1985), prohibits licensure for impersonating a licensed practitioner or permitting or allowing another to use a physician's name or certificate to practice medicine in state, or aiding or abetting, directly or indirectly, practice of medicine by any person, partnership, association, or corporation not duly licensed to practice medicine by Texas State Board of Medical Examiners

b) Illinois Medical Practice Act, § 16 (Smith-Hurd 1982–1983), prohibits:

(1) holding one's self out to treat human ailments under any name other than the physician's own
(2) impersonating any other physician
(3) having professional connection or association with, or lending one's name to another for the illegal practice by another of practice of medicine
(4) giving to or receiving from any physician, person, firm, or corporation, directly or indirectly, any fee, commission, rebate, or other form of compensation for any professional services not actually and personally rendered

D. Differentiate state attitudes
   1. Texas: "Fruits of Labor" rule—If a lay person or corporation participates in monetary rewards of a physician's medical practice, that physician must have either:
      a) permitted or allowed another to use that physician's license for the purpose of treating human beings or
      b) aided or abetted the practice of medicine by a person not duly licensed to practice medicine in the state. *See, e.g., Garcia v. Texas State Board of Medical Examiners,* 384 F.Supp. 434 (W.D. Tex. 1974), *aff'd mem.,* 421 U.S. 995 (1975);
   2. Illinois: It apparently is permissible for a hospital to employ physician, market that physician's services to the community, and participate in the financial rewards of the physician's practice of medicine
   3. West Virginia: Corporate practice of medicine prohibition struck down with respect to nonprofit corporations *Kugel v. Herbert J. Thomas Memorial Hosp. Ass'n.,* No. CA-77-3124 (W.Va. 13th Jud. Cir. Aug. 24, 1978)
   4. Wisconsin: Statute amended to provide contract exception to fee-splitting prohibition to allow combined billing by hospital if following limitations are compiled with:
      a) Physician must be a member of, or acceptable to, and subject to approval of hospital's medical staff
      b) Physician's remuneration is established
      c) Physician may exercise professional judgment without supervision or interference by hospital WIS. STAT. ANN. § 48.23(5) (West Supp. 1978–1979)

II. Fee-splitting prohibitions
   A. Prohibition typically runs only against physicians paying other physicians, not against payment by hospitals to physicians
   B. State statutes generally prohibit division of physician's fees with referral sources and payment of commission for patient referrals

C. State attitudes vary
D. Joint Committees on Accreditation of Hospitals states that medical staff bylaws must require affirmative pledge of no fee-splitting

III. Prohibition against solicitation of patients

IV. Impact on joint venture development
A. Entrepreneurs in Texas and California have devised a "captive professional corporation/association" alternative in which physician is investor in management company
B. Questions have been raised whether any activities pursued by the various joint venture entities constitute the practice of medicine.
C. American Medical Association opposes risk sharing by physicians with hospitals (e.g., DRG Incentive Venture); *see* AMA Judicial Council Report D (Ethical Implications of Hospital-Physician Risk-Sharing Arrangement Under DRGs).
1. AMA reaction spawned by *United States v. Greber,* Crim. No. 83-00414, slip op. (3rd Cir. July 10, 1985), holding that an active transaction violates Medicare fraud and abuse provisions if even part of a professional payment was intended to induce referrals
2. AMA requested investigation of physician incentive arrangement used by Hollywood Community Hospital in light of *Greber*
3. California Board of Medical Quality Assurance cleared Physicians' Sharing in Cost Savings program

CERTIFICATE OF NEED, SEC. 1122

I. CON: Similar health planning programs with different triggering levels and events
A. Section 1122 [Title II of the Social Security Act; added by P.L. 92-603 (1972); codified at 42 U.S.C. § 1320a-1]
1. Implementation
a) Any state or territory by agreement between its governor and the Secretary of HHS
b) As of 1985, there were 16 states and territories with agreements
c) Implementation of Section 1122 program currently at state's option; if capital expenditures were not built into Medicare prospective payment by October 1, 1986, all states were required to have Section 1122 programs. P.L. 98-21 [Social Security Act Amendments of 1983]

2. Triggering Event: A capital expenditure that:
   a) Exceeds $600,000, or a lesser amount as determined by a state
   b) Changes bed capacity
   c) Changes services offered substantially
3. Facilities covered
   a) Hospitals
   b) Skilled nursing facilities
   c) Intermediate care facilities
   d) HMOs under limited circumstances
   e) Others
4. Process
   a) Notice to a Designated Planning Agency ("DPA") at least 60 days prior to incurring a capital expenditure in excess of trigger amount
   b) Determination of the DPA's recommendation within 60 days, with automatic favorable recommendation if DPA fails to act within deadline
   c) Fair hearing
   d) Final determination of DPA's recommendation
   e) Determination by Secretary of HHS
   f) Request for reconsideration of adverse decision within six months
   g) Judicial review of Secretary's decision not available
5. Consequences of failure to give notice or obtain favorable determination of the Secretary
   a) Capital expenditure still may be made
   b) Denial of Medicare and Medicaid reimbursement attributable to depreciation, interest on borrowed funds, return on equity capital, and other expenses related to capital expenditure; issue: whether "other expenses" includes operating costs of providing care to Medicare/Medicaid beneficiaries
   c) No loss of licensure
6. Proposed changes in Section 1122 program.
   a) Current regulations are codified at 42 C.F.R. § 100.101.
   b) The Secretary proposed in 48 Fed. Reg. 36390 (August 10, 1983):
      (1) to repeal existing regulations entirely.
      (2) to issue new regulations to be codified at 42 C.F.R. § 125.101 et seq.; the purpose is to make Section 1122 review procedures as consistent with P.L. 93-641 CON review procedures as possible

(3) new regulations still under development

B. P.L. 93-641 (as amended) Certificate of Need Review (Title XV of the Social Security Act) codified at 42 U.S.C. § 300k et seq.

1. Federal "Model" Law
   a) Federal statute establishes a particular approach to CON review
   b) State implementation "optional":
      (1) carrot—funding to support CON review
      (2) stick—loss of federal monies under other programs
   c) CON review in a particular state pursuant to state law, not P.L. 93-641 as amended
   d) Deadline for state compliance was put off several times by Congress and future of program was in question
2. Prohibition against undertaking covered projects (CON) without state approval
3. Triggering events:
   a) Capital expenditure that:
      (1) exceeds the "expenditure minimum" ($600,000 until October 1980; thereafter states can increase it based on Commerce Department index)
      (2) changes bed capacity by
         (*a*) increasing or decreasing total number of beds
         (*b*) redistributing beds among various categories, or
         (*c*) relocating beds from one physical facility or site to another by ten beds or 10 percent of total bed capacity, whichever is less, in any two-year period
      (3) substantially changes services
   b) Acquisition of major medical equipment that:
      (1) costs more than $400,000
      (2) is owned by or located in a health care facility, or will be used for inpatient care
      (3) does not include clinical laboratory equipment independent of a doctor's office
      (4) prohibits states seeking to comply with federal model from increasing coverage of major medical equipment after September 30, 1982.
   c) Institutional health services:
      (1) provided through health care facilities
      (2) entail annual operating costs of at least $250,000 (state has been able to increase threshold after September 1980 based on Secretary of HHS-designated index)
4. "Health care" facilities usually are covered:

a) Hospitals
b) Skilled nursing facilities
c) HMOs under limited circumstances
d) Ambulatory surgery centers (in some states)

5. Notices and limited findings for certain "noncovered" projects:
   a) Acquisition of a health care facility
   b) Acquisition of major medical equipment
6. Penalties: State CON program must include sanctions (Secretary of HHS authorized to determine sufficiency of states' sanctions) such as:
   a) Injunctive relief
   b) Loss of government funds and reimbursement
   c) Denial of revocation of license
   d) Civil or criminal penalties

C. Impact on joint ventures
   1. Acquisition of equipment, modification of space, construction of facility, etc., may require CON
   2. Expenditures by "health care facilities" (e.g., hospitals) to establish joint venture may require CON
      a) New service
      b) Substantial expansion of existing service
      c) Change in services
   3. Physician's office exception often useful to avoid problems
   4. Joint ventures involving ambulatory surgery centers included in definition of "health care facilities" in most CON programs
   5. Expenditure by hospital subsidiary may be considered expenditure "on behalf of health care facility" for CON purposes

II. Rate review
   A. Objectives
      1. Reduce health care costs by:
         a) Review and approval of hospital rates prospectively
         b) Approval of only those rates necessary to meet total hospital financial requirements
      2. Regulate rates, not prices
         a) Each department has "unit of activity"
         b) Rate will be on gross volume of department
         c) Can charge more for one procedure than another but average cannot exceed rate for department
   B. Methodology
      1. Peer grouping
      2. Line item budget review

3. Interim monitoring and adjustment by hospital
4. Year-end reconciliation

LICENSURE/ACCREDITATION

I. State Licensure
   A. Applicable where purpose of joint venture is to establish/operate a facility that will provide health care services (e.g., states usually require licensure of ambulatory surgery center)
   B. Licensure requirements may differ depending upon whether the facility is hospital-affiliated or independent

II. Accreditation
   A. Joint Commission on Accreditation of Hospitals (JCAH), a voluntary organization, surveys and accredits hospitals and ambulatory care services provided by or under sponsorships of hospitals
   B. Other voluntary accrediting organizations include Accrediting Association for Ambulatory Health Care (AAAHC) and National Association of Freestanding Ambulatory Centers (NAFAC)

Appendix G

Third Party Payment: Regulatory Considerations

GENERAL COVERAGE AND PAYMENT

I. Reimbursement
   A. Coverage
   B. Certification
   C. Payment (Reimbursement)
   D. Reassignment
II. Coverage Requirements of Third Party Payers
   A. Medicare
      1. Distinction between types of covered services:
         a) Provider services—e.g., hospital services.
            (1) inpatient hospital services (42 U.S.C. § 1395x(b)).
            (2) outpatient hospital services (42 U.S.C. § 1395x(s) (2) (C)).
         b) Physicians' services (42 U.S.C. § 1395x(q)).
         c) Services incident to physician services (42 U.S.C. § 1395x(s) (2)).
         d) Others.
      2. Medicare Part A: Inpatient hospital services-scope of benefits (42 U.S.C. § 1395d): inpatient hospital services for up to 150 days during any spell of illness minus 1 day for each day of inpatient hospital services in excess of 90 received during any preceding spell of illness.
      3. Medicare Part B: Medical and other health services, Social Security Act (S.S.A.) § § 1832, 1861(s):
         a) Physicians' services
         b) Services and supplies furnished as an incident to physician's services

c) Hospital services incident to physicians' services rendered to outpatients: services customarily provided to patients by a hospital that contribute to the diagnosis or treatment of an illness or injury
d) Diagnostic services furnished to hospital outpatients
e) Outpatient physical therapy services
f) Rural health clinic services
g) Comprehensive outpatient rehabilitation facility services
h) Certain surgical procedures performed in either a qualified (1) ambulatory surgical center or (2) physician's office
i) Home health services
j) Home dialysis supplies and equipment; institutional dialysis services and supplies
k) Antigens prepared by a physician
l) Diagnostic tests
m) Therapeutic X-ray
n) Surgical dressings, splints, casts, etc.
o) Durable medical equipment used in the home
p) Ambulance services
q) Prosthetic services
r) Leg, arm, back and neck braces, and artificial legs, arms, and eyes
s) Pneumococcal vaccine

4. Other Medicare Part B Coverage
   a) Hospice Services (S.S.A. § 1861dd);
   b) Cardiac rehabilitation programs (Coverage Issues Manual § 35–25, MEDICARE & MEDICAID GUIDE (CCH) ¶ 27,201); and
   c) Cardiac catheterization (Coverage Issues Manual § 35–45).

B. Medicaid (S.S.A. § 1905[a])
1. Inpatient hospital services
2. Outpatient hospital services, including rural health clinic services
3. Laboratory and x-ray services
4. Early and periodic screening and diagnosis
5. Family planning services and supplies
6. Physicians' services
7. Medical care furnished by licensed practitioners within scope of state law practice limitations

8. Home health care services
9. Private duty nursing services
10. Clinic services
11. Dental services
12. Physical therapy and related services
13. Prescribed drugs, dentures, prosthetic devices, and prescribed eyeglasses
14. Diagnostic screening, preventive, and rehabilitative services
15. Services of nurse midwife
16. Any other medical and/or remedial care recognized under a Medicaid state plan

C. Other third party payers:
1. Scope of covered hospital and ambulatory care services of other third party payers limited by provisions of contracts with such payers; determination of scope of covered services requires examination of each such contract
2. Example: Pennsylvania Blue Shield (PBS) types of services covered
   a) Coverage for the following:
      (1) outpatient surgical care
      (2) oral surgery
      (3) radiation therapy
      (4) anesthetic services
      (5) diagnostic X-rays
      (6) diagnostic medical and pathological examinations
      (7) home and office medical care under specific circumstances
   b) Actual services covered are dependent upon specific contract with subscriber.

III. Payment

A. Medicare
1. Prospective payment system (PPS) (Social Security Amendments of 1983, P.L. 98-21, Title VI; Medicare regulations, *see* 49 Fed. Reg. 234–340 (January 3, 1984))
   a) Payment to most hospitals for Medicare Part A inpatient operating costs including:
      (1) routine services
      (2) ancillary services
      (3) intensive care
   b) Payments based upon prospectively determined rates applied on a per-discharge basis (DRG); does not apply to the following (as of mid-1986):

(1) capital costs
(2) education costs
(3) kidney acquisition costs incurred by approved hospitals
(4) outpatient costs
(5) part B inpatient costs

c) Statutory unbundling provision prohibits Medicare payment to any entity other than the hospital under either Part A or B for nonphysician services to a hospital inpatient. S.S.A. § 1862(a) (14)

2. Cost-related prospective payment systems
   a) Hospice care programs
   b) End-Stage renal disease facilities
   c) Independent rural health clinics
   d) Ambulatory surgical centers
3. Reasonable cost reimbursement (S.S.A. §§ 1814 and 1861[v]) still governs hospital outpatient services and services not governed by PPS
   a) Medicare reimbursement formula:
      (1) total allowable cost by cost center, from general ledger;
      (2) allocation of overhead cost centers to revenue-producing departments
      (3) apportionment of total allowable costs to Medicare patients—amount reimbursed
   b) Allowable cost
      (1) in absence of specific provision in regulations, manuals, or elsewhere, allowable costs are costs that are reasonable, necessary, and related to patient care.
      (2) reasonable in amount and necessary as measured in comparison with comparable facilities or measured by other criteria.
      (3) related to patient care is narrowly defined.
4. Reasonable charge reimbursement (S.S.A. §§ 1842 and 1887—method of reimbursement for physicians' services and certain nonphysician services, supplies, and equipment)
   a) Determination of reasonable charge (42 C.F.R. §§ 405.501 *et seq.*) lowest of:
      (1) actual charge made by physician or supplier
      (2) physician's or supplier's customary charge (midpoint on array of actual charges)

(3) prevailing charge by all physicians or suppliers in community—lower of
   (*a*) 75th percentile of customary charges in prior calendar year; or
   (*b*) prevailing charge determined for FYE 1973 as adjusted by economic index data, etc.
(4) comparable circumstances; or
(5) other factors that may be found necessary and appropriate in judging whether the charge is inherently reasonable (for example, an additional charge factor, the inflation indexed charge, has been added to determination of reasonable charges for certain nonphysician services, supplies and equipment (e.g., durable medical equipment, ambulance services, and prosthetic services) furnished on or after October 1, 1985. This new factor represents the lowest of the fee screens from the preceding fee screen year as updated by an inflation adjustment factor. 50 Fed. Reg. 40,168 (October 1, 1985).
(6) special limits for specific models.
   (*a*) compensation related customary charge profiles (42 C.F.R. § 405.551).
   (*b*) hospital outpatient setting. (TEFRA § 104).

b) Section 2306 of the Deficit Reduction Act of 1984 established a freeze on Medicare customary and prevailing charges for all physician services. The Consolidated Omnibus Budget Reconciliation Act was enacted on April 7, 1986, extending the Act until April 30, 1986. Effect of freeze extension on physicians:
   (1) Medicare customary and prevailing charges for physicians' services rendered during the period October 1, 1985 through April 30, 1986, remain at the level of customary and prevailing charges which were in effect through September 30, 1985.

   —effective May 1, 1986, the customary and prevailing charges will be updated for those physicians who chose to participate in the period from May 1, 1986 through December 31, 1986, regardless of their prior participation status. Only the customary charges will be updated for those physicians who participated in the period from October 1, 1984 through September 30, 1985, but chose not to participate in the 8-month period beginning May, 1986. Neither the customary nor the prevailing charges will be updated for those physicians who have never participated in the Medicare program

(2) physicians who did not choose to participate for the year beginning October 1, 1985, cannot charge, for services rendered during the period from October 1, 1985 through April 30, 1986, more than was charged in the quarter ending June 30, 1984. Additionally, those physicians who did not choose to participate during the period from May 1, 1986 through December 31, 1986, cannot charge, for services rendered during this period, more than was charged in the quarter ending June 30, 1984

(3) physicians who are currently participating in Medicare may increase their actual charges, regardless of their prior participation status

c) Reasonable charge payment procedure

(1) role of carrier—determine and pay reasonable charge for covered physician services to *or* on behalf of Medicare beneficiary (less deductible and coinsurance)

(*a*) deductible ($75 per calendar year)

(*b*) coinsurance (20 percent of reasonable charge) (with certain exceptions)

(2) claims procedure:

(*a*) beneficiary files and receives payment

(*b*) assignment option

i) Physician *may* accept assignment;

ii) Deficit Reduction Act of 1984, § 2306 created two categories of physicians/suppliers (i.e. participating—and nonparticipating): participating physician/supplier agrees to accept assignment for all services for a 12 month period

5. Implementation of 1 percent Medicare payment reduction—HCFA has issued interim Manual instructions for implementing the 1 percent reduction in Medicare payments required by the presidential sequestration order issued in compliance with the Balanced Budget and Emergency Deficit Control Act of 1985, P.L. 99–177. The 1 percent reduction

applies to PPS discharges occurring after February 28, 1986, and before October 1, 1986, and to all other services—including non-PPS inpatient hospital, outpatient hospital, SNF, HHA, CORF, renal dialysis facility, and rural health clinic—rendered after February 28, 1986, and before October 1, 1986

B. Medicaid.

1. Payments to physicians vary widely from state to state; e.g. payments may be the same as those prescribed by the Medicare program or may be based on a lower percentile than Medicare's 75th percentile or may be based on a fee schedule
2. Payments to hospitals under the Medicaid program must be at rates which "are reasonable and adequate to meet the costs which must be incurred by efficiently and economically operated facilities." S.S.A. § 1902(a)(13), codified at 42 U.S.C. § 1396a(13). P.L. 96–499 § 962(a), applicable to services furnished after October 1, 1980, removed the former requirement that payments to hospitals be made "on a reasonable cost related basis"
3. Payments to other providers under the Medicaid program must "be consistent with efficiency, economy and quality of care." S.S.A. § 1902(a)(30); 42 C.F.R. § 447.200
   a) Outpatient hospital and clinic services—the agency may not pay more than the combined payments the provider gets from the beneficiaries and carriers or intermediaries for providing comparable services under comparable circumstances under Medicare. 42 C.F.R. § 447.321.
   b) Other outpatient facilities—the agency may pay the customary charges of the provider but must not pay more than the prevailing charges in the locality for comparable services under comparable circumstances. 42 C.F.R. § 447.325

C. Other

1. Reimbursement methodologies vary. Range includes charge-based reimbursement, cost-based reimbursement, cost-related reimbursement, prospective payment, etc.

IV. Medicare and Medicaid Reassignment Prohibition and Exceptions

A. Prior to 1972, it was permissible for Medicare and Medicaid payment for physician services to be sent directly to any address and in the name of any entity designated by the physician

B. Congress, to curtail perceived abuses resulting from physician utilization of factoring companies, enacted the Medicare/Medicaid Anti-Factoring Law, P.L. 92–603 § 236, (Social Security Act § 1842(b) (5)) [codified at 42 U.S.C. §§ 1395u and 1396a(a)]. The statute provides that the carrier or intermediary may pay assigned benefits to the provider, physician or other supplier who furnished the service, and *prohibits* reassignments by a physician of assigned claims *except* to:

1. The physician's employer, if as a condition of employment, the physician is required to assign his fees to his employer
2. The facility in which the services to be reimbursed were provided if there is a contractual arrangement between the facility and the physician under which only the facility may bill for the physician's services
3. A government agency or entity
4. The physician's billing and collection agent, in the name of the physician, if
   a) An agency agreement exists;
   b) The agent's compensation is not related directly or indirectly to the dollar amounts billed or collected; and
   c) The agent's compensation is not dependent on the actual collection of payment;
5. The organized health care delivery system in which the services to be reimbursed were provided if there is a contractual arrangement between the organized health care delivery system and the physician under which only the organized health care delivery system may bill for the physician's services (42 C.F.R. § 405.1680)
6. An assignee established by court order (42 C.F.R. § 1682)

C. See HIM-14-3 § 3060 for complete statement of all exceptions and applicable criteria and conditions. MEDICARE & MEDICAID GUIDE (CCH) ¶ 11,145.

D. The statutory and regulatory language is phrased in terms of exceptions which "may be granted." HCFA may argue that it is permitted but not required to grant the above *exceptions* allowing payment to employer and facility. *See Michael Reese Physicians & Surgeons S.C. v. Quern,* 625 F.2d 764 (7th Cir. *en banc* 1980), *cert, denied,* 101 S. Ct. 860 (1981), MEDICARE & MEDICAID GUIDE (CCH) ¶ 30,576 wherein it was held that the Medicaid programs may require that each physician designate only one street address to which *all* payments would be mailed and that recognition of the statutory exceptions was within the administering agency's discretion

E. Employer–employee exception may be presumed satisfied, if alleged, in the absence of any reason for the Carrier to believe the contrary. If any question exists, whether payments to physicians are reported to the Internal Revenue Service on Form W-2 is controlling. HIM-14-3 § 3060.1.C

F. Facility exception. "Facility" in this context is limited to "institutions that make provision for furnishing services to individuals as *inpatients,* i.e., hospitals, university medical centers that own and operate hospitals, skilled nursing facilities, nursing homes, the skilled nursing facility or nursing home units of retirement homes, and other institutions of a similar nature." HIM-14-3 § 3060.2.C. If the Facility serves as *mere conduit* for physician services revenue, the Facility must have a "significant degree of control over and/or interest in the disposition of the fees" unless the conduit recipient itself would have qualified in its own right as a permissive reassignee under any of the above exceptions. HIM-14-3 § 3060.2.A

G. Health care delivery system exception. Four types of systems may qualify
   1. Carrier-dealing group practice prepayment plans.
   2. Direct-dealing group practice prepayment plans.
   3. Health maintenance organizations.
   4. Medical group clinics. To qualify as medical group clinic, the clinic must be "an organization":
      a) Which provides outpatient medical care (and ordinarily only outpatient care) in quarters which it owns or leases; and
      b) Which, if not a freestanding renal dialysis facility, is organized in one of the following ways:
         (1) as an organization in which a physician or physicians have the majority interest or
         (2) as a foundation or nonprofit corporation
      c) A freestanding renal dialysis facility may qualify to receive payment for physician services even though it is owned in whole or part by laymen and is operated for profit.
      d) For payment to be made to a clinic for physician services if the services must ordinarily be furnished within the physical premises of the clinic unless the physician is associated with the clinic as sole proprietor, partner, or employee. (This rule would not apply where the clinic may be considered to furnish the service itself under § 3060D. If the physician is associated with the clinic as

sole proprietor, partner or employee, the guidelines in § 3060D or 3060.1 control the permissibility of payment to the clinic.) HIM-14-3 § 3060.3.D

H. Example: A professional corporation may not itself qualify as a "physician" within the meaning of the Medicare prohibition against reassignment. Thus, it cannot bill and collect the professional fees of its physician members unless it qualifies within one of the exceptions to the reassignment prohibition. *Northeast Emergency Medical Associates P.C. v. Califano,* 470 F. Supp. 1111 (E.D. Pa. 1979), MEDICARE & MEDICAID GUIDE (CCH) ¶ 29,904. A professional corporation *may* qualify under either the employer–employee exception, the medical group clinic exception, or under the billing agent exception

I. Supplier. A supplier may be an individual, partnership, trust, or estate. Where the supplier is a partnership, any services furnished by a partner are considered furnished by the supplier if those services are within the scope of the partnership agreement. A statement by a physician partnership that it consistently bills in the name of the partnership for the services of its partners within the scope of the partnership agreement will establish its right to receive assigned Part B payment for those services. HIM-14 § 3060A.

CERTIFICATION, COVERAGE, AND REIMBURSEMENT FOR SPECIFIC AMBULATORY CARE VENTURES

I. Physician-Directed Clinics (Including Urgent Care Centers, Ambulatory Care Clinics and Imaging Centers)

A. The phrase "physician-directed clinic" is the Medicare terminology referring to urgent care centers, ambulatory care clinics, freestanding imaging centers, group practice associations, etc., and are typically reimbursed by Medicare on a reasonable charge basis for physicians' services and services supplied incident thereto, subject to deductibles and 20 percent coinsurance.

B. HIM-14-3 § 2050.4 defines a physician-directed clinic as one where

1. a physician (or a number of physicians) is present to perform medical rather than administrative services at all times the clinic is open
2. each patient is under the care of a clinic physician
3. the nonphysician services are under medical supervision

C. Medicare reimbursement for physicians' services
   1. Statutory (S.S.A. § 1861(q)): Professional services performed by physicians including:
      a) Surgery
      b) Consultation
      c) Home, office and institutional calls
      d) Excluding services performed in hospitals by interns and residents
   2. Regulatory [42 C.F.R. § 405.550(b)]: "The carrier will pay for services of physicians to patients of providers on a reasonable charge basis only if the following requirements are met:
      a) The services are personally furnished for an individual patient by a physician
      b) The services ordinarily require performance by a physician
      c) The services must contribute directly to the diagnosis or treatment of an individual patient
      d) In the case of anesthesiology, radiology, or laboratory services, the additional requirements in § § 405.552, 405.554, or 405.556 must be met."
   3. General instructions (HIM-14 § 2020.A): The professional services performed by a physician or physicians for a patient including diagnosis, therapy, surgery, and consultation. A service may be considered a physician's service where the physician either examines the patient in person or is able to visualize some aspect of the patient's condition without the interposition of a third person's judgment.

D. Medicare coverage and reimbursement for services and supplies furnished as an incident to physicians' services.
   1. Statutory (S.S.A. § 1861(s) (2)): Included within the term "medical and other health services" which constitute covered services under Part B of the Medicare program are certain types of services and supplies furnished "incident to a physician's service."
   2. General instructions (HIM-14-3 § 2050): Services and supplies covered under this provision are those furnished "incident to a physician's professional service" of kinds which are commonly furnished in physicians' offices (or physician-directed clinics) and are commonly *either* rendered without charge *or* included in physicians' bills. To be considered "incident to a physician's professional service" the services or

supplies must be furnished as an integral, although incidental, part of the physician's personal professional services rendered during the diagnosis or treatment of an injury or illness under the physician's direct supervision by *employees* of the physician or physician-directed clinic

3. In physician-directed clinics, where "direct supervision" may be the responsibility of several physicians, as opposed to an individual attending physician, the physician ordering a service need not be the physician who is supervising the service. However, services performed off clinic premises by clinic-employed auxiliary personnel will be covered only if performed under the direct supervision of a clinic physician. HIM-14-3 § 2050.4.

E. Medicaid coverage and reimbursement for physicians' services
   1. Statutory: No definition of the term "physicians' services" provided
   2. Regulatory (42 C.F.R. § 440.50): Services provided within State law scope of practice of medicine or osteopathy *by or under the personal supervision* of a physician or osteopath
   3. Reimbursement varies from state-to-state

F. Medicare/Medicaid coverage and reimbursement for ambulatory x-ray services and other physician-directed clinic derivatives.
   1. Medicare
      a) Coverage for "diagnostic x-ray tests" (including physician-supervised x-ray services furnished in a patient's home). S.S.A. § 1861(s) (3)
      b) Conditions for coverage of portable x-ray services, 42 C.F.R. § § 405.1411–405.1416. Includes standards for qualification of physician supervisor, orientation of technical personnel, preservation of records, safety, and inspection of equipment. Guidelines issued effective December 14, 1983 create a uniform national reimbursement methodology for portable x-ray services through a three-tier system including a professional component, a technical component, and a transportation component. HIM-14-3 § 5244
      c) Reimbursement on a reasonable charge basis under Part B of the program
      d) Freestanding imaging centers
      e) Oncology centers/radiation therapy
   2. Medicaid—*See* laboratory coverage discussed below.

II. Hospital Outpatient Departments; Medicare Limitation on Reasonable Cost and Reasonable Charge for Outpatient Services
  A. Certification
    1. Conditions for participation for outpatient departments. 42 C.F.R. § 405.1032.
    2. Medicare State Operations Manual ("HIM-7") § 2208.
    3. HIM-7 § 2208 declared obsolete in April 1980 upon publication of HCFA-Pub. 7.
    4. Hospitals desiring to claim a facility as an outpatient department must so designate on annual HCFA 1514 survey form.
  B. Coverage
    1. Medicare: Normal coverage for hospital outpatient services and physicians' services to patients.
    2. Medicaid: Normal coverage for hospital outpatient services and physicians' services to patients.
  C. Reimbursement
    1. Medicare.
      a) Hospital outpatient services.
        (1) reimbursement under Part B for 80 percent of the reasonable cost of all services and supplies provided by the hospital in connection with the treatment of outpatients, except outpatient clinical diagnostic laboratory services. Clinical diagnostic laboratory tests performed by a hospital lab for hospital outpatients are reimbursed pursuant to fee schedules established at 62 percent of the prevailing charge level. Such fee schedules will apply during the period beginning on July 1, 1984. Deficit Reduction Act of 1984, § 2302
        (2) deficit Reduction Act of 1984, § 2308 eliminated ability to combine inpatient and outpatient charges for purpose of avoiding LCC limitation problem
      b) Physician services to patients
        (1) reasonable charge reimbursement for physicians' services subject to deductibles and 20 percent co-insurance.
        (2) provider based physician regulations.
        (3) TEFRA § 104, (P.L. 97-35 § 2142 (1982): Limitation on reasonable charge for physicians' services furnished in hospital outpatient settings
          (*a*) applicable to physicians' services furnished in

hospital outpatient settings that are *routinely* provided in a physician's office

(*b*) carrier has broad discretion in establishing list of services to which limit will apply

(*c*) physicians' services excluded from limits:
—rural health clinic services
—ambulatory surgical services
—bona fide emergency department services—Sec. 2318 of Deficit Reduction Act of 1984 provides that "bona fide emergency services" means service provided in a hospital emergency department after the sudden onset of a medical condition manifesting itself by acute symptoms of sufficient severity such that the absence of immediate medical attention could reasonably be expected to result in (a) placing the patient's health in serious jeopardy; (b) serious impairment to bodily functions; or (c) serious dysfunction of any bodily organ or part;
—anesthesiology services
—diagnostic and therapeutic radiology services
—physician services paid on compensation-related customary charge profile basis
—situations where duplicate payments could not occur (Preamble)

(*d*) charge base defined as Office-Based, *Non-specialist* prevailing charge profile (However, Sixth Circuit Court recently invalidated the regulation authorizing the establishment of separate prevailing charge screens for specialists and non-specialists. The court held that the regulation was irrational and that the Medicare Act did not authorize the establishment of separate screens for similar services based upon a physician's specialty status. *Michigan Academy of Family Physicians v. BC/BS of Michigan,* MEDICARE & MEDICAID GUIDE (CCH) ¶ 33,632 *aff'd, Bowen v. Michigan Academy of Family Physicians,* 54 U.S.L.W. 4594 (June 9, 1986)

(*e*) calculation of limit—60 percent of charge base.

(*f*) application of limit—reasonable charge is the lowest of

i) actual charge
ii) provider setting customary charge profile
iii) provider setting prevailing charge profile
iv) outpatient charge limit

(4) special teaching physician reimbursement rules.
(*a*) I.L. 372.
i) personally performed physician services
ii) "attending physician" status
(*b*) Adopted into law by P.L. 96-449 § 948. MEDICARE & MEDICAID GUIDE (CCH) ¶ 24,131
(*c*) Deficit Reduction Act of 1984, § 2307 revised formula for calculating teaching physicians' customary charges by providing that customary charges cannot be less than 85% of prevailing charges in same locality. § 2307 also provides that, as an alternative method for computing teaching physician reasonable charges, if all the "teaching physicians" at a particular teaching hospital agree to take assignment for all Medicare patients served in that hospital, the customary charge will be set at 90 percent of the prevailing charge.

2. Medicaid
a) Outpatient hospital services and clinic services
b) upper limits of payment: the agency may not pay more than the combined payments the provider gets from the beneficiaries and carries or intermediaries for providing comparable services under comparable circumstances under Medicare. 42 C.F.R. § 447.321. Thus, § 104 of TEFRA is indirectly applicable to the Medicaid program
3. Other (e.g., certain Blue Cross Plans exclude from coverage routine care and diagnostic services)
4. Reimbursement for physician administrative services furnished in hospital outpatient department subject to Reasonable Compensation Equivalents (RCEs)
5. Maximizing reimbursement for ambulatory care services if furnished in hospital outpatient department
a) Identify and evaluate current ambulatory care services
(1) determine profitability of outpatient clinics
(2) perform analysis of cost accounting system
(3) identify alternative sources of funding for ambulatory care services

b) Assess organization of ambulatory care delivery
   (1) determine efficiency of current organization
   (2) evaluate benefits of alternative ambulatory care delivery modes (e.g., establishment of outpatient surgical clinic as an "independent" ambulatory surgical center)

c) Analyze cost reimbursement data
   (1) in post-prospective payment era, rethink strategies concerning cost allocations between hospital inpatient and outpatient cost centers
   (2) explore alternative, more sophisticated cost allocation methodologies
   (3) initiate review of alternative statistical bases for cost allocation of support and ancillary services costs (e.g., hours of service versus square footage, direct costing, etc.)
   (4) initiate periodic review of cost allocation methodologies

III. Comparison of Hospital Outpatient Department and Physician-Directed Clinic

A. Perform detailed financial analysis/feasibility study to compare financial results available under hospital outpatient department and physician-directed clinic certification and reimbursement alternatives. Focus on revenue comparisons since expenses can be assumed to remain constant in short-term (although expenses could be reallocated among the parties depending on model selected).

IV. Ambulatory Surgical Centers. See ASC Case Study p.8-1

A. Certification

1. Conditions for coverage delineated in regulation 42 C.F.R. Part 416 (42 Fed. Reg. 34,082). Standards for the following are included:

a) Compliance with state licensure law
b) Governing body and management
c) Surgical services
d) Evaluation of quality
e) Environment
f) Medical staff
g) Nursing services
h) Medical records
i) Pharmaceutical services
j) Laboratory and radiological services

2. All of the above certification conditions may be deemed fulfilled if the surgical center:
   a) Is accredited by a national accrediting body (although no national body has as yet been approved to grant such accreditation)
   b) Meets any state licensing requirements
   c) Releases accreditation survey to HCFA. 42 C.F.R. § 416.39

B. Coverage
   1. Medicare: S.S.A. § 1832(a)(2)(F).
   2. List of covered surgical procedures contained in 47 Fed. Reg. 34099, MEDICARE & MEDICAID (CCH) ¶ 20,875AA.

C. Reimbursement.
   1. Prior law regarding Medicare reimbursement for surgical procedures.
      a) Physicians' services: 80 percent of the reasonable charge for the surgical procedure, regardless of the setting in which the surgery was performed.
      b) Facility costs: 100 percent of the reasonable cost if performed in a hospital on an inpatient basis; 80 percent of the reasonable cost if the surgery was performed in a hospital outpatient department located on hospital campus or at satellite location; no reimbursement if performed in a non-hospital related (independent) setting
   2. Effect of 1980 Amendments (Omnibus Reconciliation Act of 1980, P.L. 96-499 § 934).
      a) Purpose of Amendments is to encourage the performance in an ambulatory setting of certain surgical procedures (those which are appropriately and safely performable in an ambulatory setting) which would otherwise be furnished on an inpatient hospital basis
      b) The Amendments authorize the Secretary to establish regulations and to provide a list of designated surgical procedures which can safely be performed in certain ambulatory surgical settings
      c) Amendments make no change with respect to cost reimbursement for surgical procedures performed in hospital-based ambulatory surgical settings (*but see* Regulations, below)
      d) With respect to surgical procedures performed in an independent setting, Amendments provide 100 percent reimbursement for "facility services" (in addition to

reimbursement for physicians' services) reimbursable on the basis of an all-inclusive rate called the "standard overhead amount" to be determined by the Secretary for each covered procedure. Center must agree to accept assignment of all Medicare claims for facility services

e) Physicians' services, and services incident thereto, which are performed in a free-standing ambulatory surgical center, the outpatient department of a hospital, or a physician's office are to be reimbursed 100% of the Medicare reasonable charge if the physician agrees to accept assignment for all services to individual patients

3. Final Regulations, 42 C.F.R. Parts 405 and 416, 42 Fed. Reg. 34,082; issued August 5, 1982
   a) As issued, regulations pertain only to certain surgical services furnished in a qualified independent ambulatory surgical center or in a hospital-affiliated ambulatory surgical center that has elected to be covered under this provision; regulations do not deal with ambulatory surgical services furnished in a physician's private office
   b) Reimbursement method for facility services based upon a prospectively determined rate per procedure. The rate is derived from a four group classification system with all procedures within each group reimbrused at a single rate, as adjusted for geographic variations. Payments per classification are as follows:

   Group 1—$231
   Group 2—$275
   Group 3—$296
   Group 4—$336

   See Attachment VI-B of Outline for list for surgical procedures covered under each Group
   c) HCFA is currently revising list of covered procedures
4. Medicare billings for "independent" ambulatory surgical center facility and physicians' services charges will be processed by area Medicare Part B *carriers.* Part A/B I.L. Nos. 82-19/82-14, Oct. 1982, CCH ¶ 32,238.
5. Considerations in establishment of independent ambulatory surgical center
   a) Facility must be a separately identifiable entity, physi-

cally, administratively, and financially independent and distinct from other operations of hospital

b) One time option "out"—once hospital elects to participate in Medicare as an independent ambulatory surgical facility cannot change to participation as component of hospital without HCFA approval

V. Independent Laboratories

A. Certification: 42 C.F.R. § § 405.1310 405.1317—Lab must be independent of both an attending and consulting physician's office and of any hospital

1. Criteria to distinguish a "hospital laboratory" from an "independent laboratory."

a) Which entity staffs the laboratory

b) Which entity pays the technicians

c) Who owns the equipment

d) Arrangements between laboratory and hospital's medical staff

e) Relationship between pathologists and hospital

B. Coverage

1. Medicare [S.S.A. § 1861(s)(3)]

a) 42 C.F.R. § 405.232(b): Covered diagnostic tests must not be performed in a laboratory which is independent of a hospital and the attending or consulting physician's office unless the laboratory meets the requirements of 42 C.F.R. § § 405.1310–405.1317 "Conditions for Coverage of Services of Independent Laboratories" which include:

(1) compliance with state and local laws

(2) qualified direction and supervision

(3) qualified staff

(4) adequate management policies

(5) adequate space, facilities, equipment

(6) compliance with safety requirements

(7) establishment of quality control procedures

b) General Instructions (HIM-14-3 § 2070)

c) Note absence of "incident to physician's service" requirement

d) Independent laboratory physiological services. Payment may be made for diagnostic physiological services, including long-term ECG and EEG diagnostic services, furnished by independent laboratories if:

(1) the laboratory meets applicable state and local licensure laws;

(2) the diagnostic services are ordered by a referring physician; and

(3) the services are determined by the carrier to be "reasonable and necessary."

Part B Intermediary Letter, No. 79-19 (May, 1979); MEDICARE & MEDICAID GUIDE (CCH) ¶ 29,728.

(4) if the laboratory furnishes only physiological services and not clinical laboratory services, the physiological laboratory does not have to meet the Medicare conditions of participation for independent laboratories

2. Medicaid [S.S.A. § 1905(a)(3)]
   a) Coverage for "outpatient hospital services," S.S.A. § 1905(a)(2) and "other laboratory and X-ray services," S.S.A. § 1905(a)(3)
   b) "Outpatient hospital services" includes "diagnostic . . . services that are furnished to outpatients. . . ." 42 C.F.R. § 440.20
   c) "Other laboratory and x-ray services" includes physician-ordered and supervised services *or* physician-ordered and billed services performed in an office or facility other than a hospital outpatient department by a laboratory that meets the Medicare conditions of participation. 42 C.F.R. § 440.30

C. Reimbursement-Deficit Reduction Act of 1984, § 2303
   1. Establishment of fee schedule at 60 percent of prevailing charges; fee screen year beginning July 1, 1984
   2. Acceptance of assignment from Medicare beneficiary mandatory
   3. Payment equal to 100 percent of fee screen amount of charge, whichever is lower (deductible and coinsurance requirements waived)
   4. Payment made only to entity or person performing or supervising performance of services, except in case of test performed at request of laboratory by another laboratory, payment may be made to referring laboratory

D. 1985 Update—fee schedules increased approximately 3 to 4 percent

E. The Consolidated Omnibus Budget Reconciliation Act of 1985 was recently enacted and will:
   1. Set a ceiling at 115% of the median fee beginning on July 1, 1986 and 110% of the median fee beginning on January 1, 1988

2. Establish a national fee schedule that would go into effect on January 1, 1988
3. Establish that Medicare payments for laboratory services performed in a physician's office be made on same basis as payments to independent laboratories, beginning on January 1, 1987

VI. Comprehensive Outpatient Rehabilitation Facility Services

A. Certification

1. Medicare conditions of participation: Regulations 42 C.F.R. § § 405.260–262
   a) Required minimum services
      (1) physicians' services
      (2) physical therapy services
      (3) social or psychological services
   b) Services must be provided under supervision of at least one physician with at least one year experience or training in the medical management of patients requiring rehabilitation services

B. Coverage.

1. Preexisting Medicare Part B coverage for ambulatory rehabilitation services
   a) Rehabilitation services furnished "incident to" a physician's professional services. S.S.A. § § 1832(a)(1); 1861(s)(2)
   b) Outpatient physical therapy and outpatient speech therapy where furnished by a provider, clinic, rehabilitation agency, public health agency. S.S.A. § § 1832(a)(2)(c), 1861(p)
   c) Other covered hospital outpatient services.
2. S.S.A. § § 1832(a)(2)(E) and 1861(bb)
3. Regulations issued by HHS on December 15, 1982, 42 C.F.R. § § 405.260–262, implementing P.L. 96–499 § 933
   a) Expands the scope of Medicare Part B benefits to include services furnished by comprehensive outpatient rehabilitation facilities (CORFs)
   b) A CORF is "a nonresidential facility that is established and operated exclusively for the purpose of providing diagnostic, therapeutic, and restorative services to outpatients for the rehabilitation of injured, disabled, or sick persons, at a single fixed location, by or under the supervision of a physician . . . " 42 C.F.R. § 488.51
   c) A CORF need not be a freestanding facility but if con-

tained within a physical structure already housing a certified facility, it must be separately certified and be functionally and operationally independent

d) Requirements for coverage
   (1) referral to CORF for treatment by a physician
   (2) coverage limited to those individuals who have significant potential for restoration or improvement of lost or impaired functions
   (3) physician must establish and periodically review the plan of treatment
   (4) all services provided by CORF must be on CORF premises except one home visit allowed to evaluate potential benefit of home rehabilitation
   (5) beneficiary must be under care of physician at all times during treatment

e) Items and services covered
   (1) physicians' services
   (2) physical therapy services
   (3) occupational therapy services
   (4) speech-language pathology services
   (5) respiratory therapy services
   (6) prosthetic and orthotic devices
   (7) social services
   (8) psychological services (Limited to lesser of $312.50 or 62½ percent of expenses)
   (9) nursing care
   (10) drugs, biologicals, supplies, appliances, and equipment
   (11) home environment evaluation

C. Reimbursement
   1. Reasonable cost reimbursement; same rules as are applicable to other providers
   2. Subject to Part B deductible; in addition, a CORF may charge a beneficiary an amount not to exceed 20 percent of its customary charges for items and services furnished. Thus, payment to CORF based upon lesser of (a) 80 percent of the reasonable cost of services, or (b) the reasonable cost of services furnished, less 20% of customary charges
   3. Payment for physician services is limited to 60 percent of the reasonable charge (based on data indicating 40 percent of a physician's gross revenues goes toward overhead costs)

VII. Cardiac Rehabilitation Programs (Coverage Issues Manual § 35-25)

A. Medicare coverage available effective September 15, 1982 for reasonable and necessary exercise programs for cardiac patients (cardiac rehabilitation programs) on behalf of certain qualifying patients furnished in either hospital outpatient departments or physician-directed clinics
B. Covered services include stress testing, electrocardiogram rhythm strips, and certain other diagnostic and therapeutic services when such services satisfy the usual coverage requirements such as "reasonable and necessary," "incident to a physician's professional services," etc.
C. Certain limitations on coverage include requirements that:
   1. If furnished in a freestanding clinic, it must be "physician-directed," i.e. a physician must be on the premises available to perform medical duties at all times the facility is open and each patient must be under the care of a hospital or clinic physician
   2. All "medically necessary" life saving equipment must be available for immediate use
   3. The program must be conducted in an area set aside for the exclusive use of the program while in session
   4. Services of nonphysician personnel must be under "direct supervision" of a physician
   5. Nonphysician personnel must be employees of the physician, hospital, or clinic conducting the program (and coverage is only available for services of these employees "incident to a physician's professional services")

VIII. Freestanding Cardiac Catheterization Facility (Coverage Issues Manual § 35-45)
A. Cardiac catheterization performed in a freestanding clinic is a Medicare covered service if the carrier determines that the procedure can be appropriately and safely performed in the clinic
B. As a practical matter, carrier approval is difficult to obtain and has been granted only infrequently

IX. End Stage Renal Disease (ESRD) Program
A. Certification
   1. Types of ESRD facilities
      a) Renal transplantation center
      b) Renal dialysis center
      c) Renal dialysis facility
      d) Self-dialysis unit
      e) Special purpose renal dialysis facility

      42 C.F.R. § 405.2102(e)
   2. Conditions for coverage set out in 42 C.F.R. Part 405

Subpart U, MEDICARE & MEDICAID GUIDE (CCH) ¶ 20,866 *et seq.*

a) General requirements for *all* ESRD facilities. See 42 C.F.R. § 405.2130–405.2140
   (1) minimal utilization rates
   (2) provider status (if hospital-operated)
   (3) fulfillment of service needs in ESRD network
   (4) furnishing data and information for ESRD program administration
   (5) membership in ESRD network
   (6) compliance with federal, state, and local laws and regulations
   (7) governing body and management
   (8) patient long-term program and patient care plan
   (9) patients' rights and responsibilities
   (10) medical records
   (11) physical environment

b) Additional special requirements for ESRD facilities furnishing dialysis services. 42 C.F.R. § 405.2160 through 405.2163. Effective May 11, 1983.
   (1) affiliation agreement or arrangement
   (2) director of renal dialysis center or renal dialysis facility
   (3) staff of renal dialysis center or renal dialysis facility
   (4) minimum service requirements

c) Conditions for coverage for special purpose renal dialysis facilities set out at 42 C.F.R. § 405.2164—includes all requirements listed above except *a*(3), *a*(5), and *a*(8)

d) Requirements for renal transplantation centers. 42 C.F.R. § 405.2170 and 405.2171.
   (1) director
   (2) minimal service requirements

B. Coverage

1. Medicare [S.S.A. § 1881]

   a) All Part A and Part B items and services, not just those associated with ESRD

   b) ESRD covered items and services (See also 42 C.F.R. § 405.2102(f) and § § 405.231(o), (p), and (q)
      (1) institutional dialysis services and supplies (including self-dialysis in a self-care dialysis unit) S.S.A. § 1881(b)(10) and 42 C.F.R. § 405.231, MEDICARE & MEDICAID GUIDE (CCH) ¶ 18,632

(2) transplantation services (including services to donors—S.S.A. § 1881(d))
(3) self-care home dialysis support services—S.S.A. § 1881(b)(9)
(4) routine professional services performed by a physician
(5) home dialysis supplies and equipment—S.S.A. § 1881(b)(8)

2. Medicaid [42 C.F.R. § 441.40]
   a) Coverage is not mandated but federal financial participation is available for facility treatment if states so elect, but only if facility has been approved to furnish those services under Medicare. Exception exists for emergency conditions as permitted under Medicare (see 42 C.F.R. § 405.1011)

C. Reimbursement
   1. Reimbursement to ESRD facilities effective August 1, 1983: Prospective payment method. 42 C.F.R. § 405.439, MEDICARE & MEDICAID GUIDE (CCH) ¶ 32,865. Rate methodology differentiates between hospital-based and independent facilities
      a) Payment rates established annually by HCFA; HCFA or intermediary will notify each facility annually as to its payment rate. Revisions in payment rate will take into account revised cost data and geographic labor cost adjustments. 42 C.F.R. § 405.440(i)
      b) Criteria for qualifying for hospital-based facility rate set out at 42 C.F.R. § 405.439(a)(3) and (4)
      c) Amount of payment will be 80 percent of prospective payment rate (PPR) after full deductible subtracted. 42 C.F.R. § 405.439(d)
      d) Bad debts paid up to facility's allowable cost in single lump sum at end of cost reporting period. 42 C.F.R. § 405.439(d)
      e) Exceptions to PPRs, 42 C.F.R. § 405.439(f) and (g)
         (1) 180-day application period after notification of PPR.
         (2) criteria for approval of exception requests
            (*a*) atypical service intensity (patient mix)
            (*b*) isolated essential facility
            (*c*) education costs
            (*d*) extraordinary circumstances

(*e*) self-dialysis training costs
(*f*) frequency of dialysis

f) HCFA has recently proposed changes in the methodology used to determine the prospective payment rates applicable to ESRD facilities furnishing outpatient maintenance dialysis services. The effect of the revised methodology, together with updated cost data and wage index information, will result in decreased average payment rates. 51 Fed. Reg. 17537 (May 13, 1986); MEDICARE & MEDICAID GUIDE (CCH) ¶ 35,383

2. Reimbursement for physicians' services
   a) Effective August 1, 1983: Physician monthly capitation method. 42 C.F.R. § 405.542(c)
   b) Factors in determining monthly payment amount include program experience and the charging practices of comparable physicians for comparable services. Factors will be reviewed periodically and updated. 42 C.F.R. § 405.542(c)(3)
   c) Extra payment, based upon reasonable charge principles, is available for declotting of shunts and for certain other categories of physician services. 42 C.F.R. § 405.542(c)(1)
   d) Monthly payments are reduced for the portion of time in which (1) the patient is hospitalized or (2) patient is not attended by the physician. 42 C.F.R. § 405.542(c)(2)

D. Proposed reorganization of ESRD network organizations—HCFA is currently proposing to restructure ESRD network organizations to improve their efficiency and remove unnecessary requirements. The proposed amendments would reduce the 32 existing network organizations to as few as 14, the minimum number permitted by Section 9214 of the Consolidated Omnibus Budget Reconciliation Act of 1985. Current networks would be given 90 days to phase out their operations, and the new organizations would be selected under a competitive contracting process. *See* 51 Fed. Reg. 12714 (Apr. 15, 1986); MEDICARE & MEDICAID GUIDE (CCH) ¶ 35,349

X. Home Health Services

A. Certification

1. Conditions for participation as a home health agency
   a) Compliance with state and local laws
   b) Organization, services, and administration
   c) Group of professional personnel

d) Acceptance of patients, plan of treatment, medical supervision
e) Skilled nursing services
f) Therapy services
g) Medical social services
h) Home health aide services
i) Clinical records
j) Evaluation
k) Qualifying to provide outpatient physical therapy services

42 C.F.R. Part 405, Subpart L, MEDICARE & MEDICAID GUIDE (CCH) ¶ 20,075 *et seq*

2. Higher conditions for participation in certain states. 42 C.F.R. Part 405, Subpart L, Appendix

B. Coverage
1. Medicare: S.S.A. § 1861(o)
a) Part A and Part B: identical features and requirements with no limit on number of covered visits.
b) Conditions for coverage (42 C.F.R. § 405.233 *et seq.*)
(1) patient confined to home
(2) under care of a physician
(3) in need of skilled nursing services or physical or speech therapy on intermittent basis
(4) on a visiting basis
(5) with a written plan of care established
(6) furnished by a home health agency or another "under arrangements"
(7) services furnished in patient's home or on an outpatient basis under certain circumstances
c) Physician certification requirements (42 C.F.R. § 405.1633)
(1) physician must certify the need for the covered service and recertify the need at least every two months
(2) certifying physician must not have a "significant financial or contractual relationship" with the home health agency (defined as a relationship involving direct or indirect business transactions with the agency involving in a given fiscal year more than $25,000 or 5 per cent of the agency's total operating expenses)

d) Items and services covered (42 C.F.R. § 405.236)
  (1) part-time or intermittent nursing care
  (2) physical, speech, or occupational therapy
  (3) medical social services
  (4) part-time or intermittent services of home health aide
  (5) medical supplies (other than drugs and biologicals), equipment and appliances.

2. Medicaid (42 C.F.R. § 440.70 and § 441.15)
  a) Mandatory services
    (1) part-time or intermittent nursing services
    (2) home health aide services
    (3) medical supplies, equipment and appliances
  b) Optional services: physical therapy, occupational therapy or speech pathology and audiology services
  c) Individuals required to be served
    (1) categorically needy; and
    (2) medically needy.

C. Reimbursement
  1. Reasonable cost basis for costs related to patient care. Prov. Reim. Man. Part 1, § 2113 *et seq*
    a) Home health coordination costs
    b) Visiting costs
    c) Medical supply costs
    d) Contracted services purchased by home health agency
  2. Reasonable cost of items and services furnished by outside supplier "under arrangements." 42 C.F.R. § 405.432.
  3. Reasonable cost subject to cap—cap on home health agency cost reimbursement set at 75th percentile of costs for free-standing home health agencies; hospital-based home health agencies receive an "add-on adjustment" to account for higher A&G costs produced by Medicare hospital cost finding requirements, 42 C.F.R. § 405.460

XI. Rural Health Clinics
  A. Certification-Conditions for participation—42 C.F.R. § 481.1 *et seq.* Key requirement for qualifying as a rural health clinic is that facility is located in a "rural area" which has been designated a shortage area for either personal health services or medical care manpower. 42 C.F.R. § 481.2. With certain exceptions, a rural area is an area not delineated as an urbanized area in the last census.

B. Coverage.

1. Medicare: S.S.A. § § 1832(a)(2)(D) and 1861(aa); 42 C.F.R. § § 405.2401 *et seq.* Covered services include physicians' services, nurse practitioner or physician assistant services (as specified in regulations), services and supplies furnished incident to such services, and visiting nurse services. 42 C.F.R. § 405.2411
2. Medicaid: S.S.A. § 1902(a)(13)(B). Covered services include those of a physician; if not prohibited by state law from furnishing primary health care and if furnished in accordance with 42 C.F.R. § 405.2414, nurse practitioner, nurse midwife, or other specialized nurse practitioner services; services and supplies furnished incident to above-related services; and certain other services. 42 C.F.R. § 440.20

C. Reimbursement

1. Medicare
   a) Covered physicians' services performed outside the clinic are reimbursable either (1) to the clinic as a rural health clinic service, if physician is *compensated* by the clinic, or (2) to the patient (or physician if assignment is accepted) on reasonable charge basis, if physician is *not compensated* by clinic
   b) All services performed at clinic
      (1) "provider" clinics are reimbursable under the basic "reasonable cost" principles applicable to other providers of services
      (2) "independent" rural health clinics are reimbursed on the basis of an all-inclusive rate for each beneficiary visit for covered services
2. Medicaid
   a) Medicaid program must pay for rural health clinic services as follows:
      (1) for provider clinics—reasonable cost reimbursement
      (2) nonprovider clinics that do not offer ambulatory care services other than rural health clinic services: reasonable cost rate per visit as determined by 42 C.F.R. § § 405.2426 through 405.2429
      (3) nonprovider clinics that offer other ambulatory care services: single rate per visit *or* rate set by agency for each service: 42 C.F.R. § 447.371

XII. Community Health Centers ("CHCs")

A. Certification—"Community health center" means an entity which, through its staff and supporting resources or through contracts or cooperative arrangements with other public or private entities, provides for all residents of its catchment area the following services: 42 C.F.R. § 51c.102(c)(1)

1. Primary health services
2. Supplemental health services necessary for the adequate support of primary health services
3. Referral to providers of supplemental health services and payment
4. Environmental health services
5. Information on the availability and proper use of health services

B. Coverage: Medicare and Medicaid. Coverage for CHCs that are determined to be physician-directed clinics is on same basis as for other physician-directed clinics (but *see,* Medicare Regional Letter No. 80-29, discussed below); provider-controlled CHCs are subject to same coverage requirements as hospital outpatient departments. Part A I.L. 73-9; MEDICARE & MEDICAID GUIDE (CCH) ¶ 3115.15

C. Reimbursement/Funding

1. Grants—P.L. 97-35 § 901 (42 U.S.C. § 300y-1), effective October 1, 1981, authorized funding for grants to community health centers in the amounts of $302.5 million for FY 1983 and $327 million for FY 1984
2. Medicare reimbursement is available for physicians' services and services furnished incident thereto. Facility may choose between two methods of reimbursement
    a) Reasonable charge reimbursement
    b) If qualifying, an all-inclusive charge related to reasonable cost. Medicare Regional Letter No. 80-29, July, 1980; MEDICARE & MEDICAID GUIDE (CCH) ¶ 3190.125

KEY TO ALPHABET SOUP

AAA— Assumed Allocation Agreement
AC— Actual Charge
CCP— Customary Charge Profile (based on mid-point of identified actual charges)
CMP— Comprehensive Medical Plan
CR-CCP— Compensation Related Customary Charge Profile (based on compensation the physician receives instead of the physician's identified actual charges)
DME— Durable Medical Equipment
HCFA— Health Care Financing Administration
HMO— Health Maintenance Organization
OIG— Office of Inspector General
OMB— Office of Budget Management
OPI/OPV—Office of Program Integrity/Office of Program Validation
PBP— Provider-Based Physician (Physician receiving compensation from the Provider or another entity for services furnished in the Provider)
PCC— Physician Compensation Cost
PCP— Prevailing Charge Profile (lower of the 75th percentile of CCPs for the last calendar year or 75th percentile of CCPs for 1973 adjusted by economic index)
PPS— Prospective Payment System
PRRB— Provider Reimbursement Review Board
PSNr— Physician Service Nonreimbursable
PSPa— Physician Service to Patient
PSPr— Physician Service to Provider
RCE— Reasonable Compensation Equivalent
WAA— Written Allocation Agreement

Appendix H

Joint Venture Glossary

Affiliated Hospital—a hospital affiliated in some way with another medical, educational, or health program, usually a medical school. Some definitions limit the term to only hospitals with close or extensive affiliations with medical schools.

Affiliation—an agreement (usually formal) between two or more independent institutions, programs, or individuals which defines how they will relate to each other. Affiliations agreements may specify the following: procedures for referring or transferring patients from one facility to another; joint faculty and/or medical staff appointments; teaching relationships; records or services; or provision of consultation between programs.

Alcohol and/or Drug Detoxification Unit—a supportive medical and health oriented environment that offers medical supervision, housing, and counseling to persons who are dependent upon alcohol and drugs. Substance withdrawal is accomplished with the aid of medications and psychological therapy.

Alliance, Regional—a formal agreement between several hospitals and/or hospital systems for specific purposes. These arrangements usually operate under a set of bylaws or other written regulations.

Ambulatory Care Center, Freestanding—a facility that offers medical care on an outpatient basis. There are about 1,000 to 2,000 freestanding ambulatory care centers. Approximately 25 percent of the freestanding centers are directly associated with hospitals.

Ambulatory Surgery Center, Freestanding—a facility offering outpatient surgery for patients who do not need to stay overnight in a hospital. Freestanding units are separate legally and usually physically from the hospital. They may include private physicians' offices. *Synonym:* Surgicenter.

Ambulatory Surgery, Hospital—a hospital based service providing minor elective surgical procedures by admitting and discharging patients on the day of surgery. Such programs are generally considered to reduce hospital costs. *Synonym:* Short Stay Surgery, Short Procedures Unit, Same Day Surgery, Come and Go Surgery, Outpatient Surgery, and One Day Surgery.

Bank—a broad and comprehensive term encompassing a variety of different kinds of financial institutions which perform one or more of the following functions: deposits, investments, loans, and other financial services.

Bankruptcy—the condition judged by a court that a debtor is insolvent. When the debtor brings the actions himself or herself, it is referred to as a voluntary bankruptcy. When the action is brought by his or her creditors it is referred to as involuntary bankruptcy.

Break Even—that point in operating a business or activity when there is neither a profit or loss generated from the business. This is called the break even point.

Business Coalitions for Health Care—association of companies developed to study a broad scope of health care issues relating to employees and employers.

Business Plan—the document and process completed and gone through in order to provide a scope of understanding and feasibility and a new program on new business. Elements of a business plan include: details about environmental assessments, operations, organization, financials, and marketing issues.

Capital Stock—capital (funds) primarily invested in a corporation or business by the owners. Capital stock is divided into shares which are issued by the owners.

Certificate of Need (CON)—a certificate that is issued by the state to an individual or organization proposing to construct or modify a health facility or to offer a new or different health service. In the certificate of need process, the Health System Agency or the local Health Planning Agency makes recommendations to the state. CON is mandated as part of Public Law 93-641. The purpose of the CON law is to ensure that services, facilities, and organizations initiated are needed. Certificate of Need laws vary from state to state.

Consolidation—individuals, organizations, institutions, or multihospital systems that form a new entity by combining two or more organizations.

Consortium—(1) Formal membership organization/arrangement that functions under a set of bylaws or other written rules to which each member agrees to abide. It may or may not be incorporated. The control of assets also resides with each member although some freedom to act independently may be prescribed in the organization's bylaws. (2) When a group of hospitals agree to multiple affiliations, this often includes shared services (for example, two hospitals sharing a clinical laboratory or a laundry service).

Corporate Restructuring—regrouping of the established hospital corporate hierarchy by creating holding companies or foundations in order to guard assets, accomplish a broader mission and effectiveness, enlarge cash flow, and permit capital accumulation. *Synonym:* Corporate Reorganization.

Corporation—a legal entity consisting of one or more persons treated in many ways as a natural person. There are various types of corporations.

Diversification—a formal strategy whereby hospitals or businesses expand functions through setting up different corporations, limited partnerships, foundations, and joint ventures to offer services. *Synonym:* Corporate Diversification.

Durable Medical Equipment (DME)—medical equipment having a useful life of one year or more but not necessarily capital equipment. This equipment is often ordered by a physician for a patient's use at home. Common illustrations of DME include: wheelchairs, walkers/canes, home respirators.

Emergency Center, Freestanding—a facility structured, equipped and staffed to offer primary, urgent, and emergency medical services. These facilities often offer laboratory and radiographic services. They often have transfer agreements for sending severely ill patients needing hospital care once the patients are stable. *Synonyms:* Urgent Care Centers; Urgi Centers; Primary Care Centers; Freestanding Emergency Center (FEC).

Entrepreneur—a person who assumes responsibilities of planning, development, and assumption of some risk for a business venture.

Equity—those interests in a company of an owner (e.g. money) as compared to those interests in a company of a creditor.

Going Public—offering to the public of shares of stock in a company in order to raise funds for the business.

Health Care Coalitions—regional or local organizations that deal with health problems normally involving the reduction of health care expenditures. The American Hospital Association's (AHA) Directory of Health Care Coalitions in the United States lists 182 coalitions which have a varied membership of representatives from business, hospitals, government, community organizations, labor and the insurance industry, and physicians. The groups' functions include data collection, health education and promotion projects and design of employee health benefit plans.

Health Maintenance Organization (HMO)—an organization that agrees to provide medical, hospital, emergency, and preventive health care in return for a prepaid membership. There are two fundamental types of HMO plans: The Group model (where HMOs contract with several group practices and share the risk of the venture with the physicians) and the Independent Practice Associations (IPA) (a loose-knit type of prepaid plan where an IPA contracts with solo physicians who see patients in their offices, often on a fee-for-service basis).

Holding Company—a separate corporate and legal entity/organization used by health care organizations and other buisnesses for a variety of reasons, among them to react to opportunities in the market place. Hospitals form holding companies by a process of corporate reorganization. *Synonym:* Foundation; parent company.

Home Care Agency—formal establishments or agencies that have facilities and offer or coordinate in home medical services including nursing services and other professional and technical services. These agencies provide treatment for patients who have specified medical conditions in their places of residence. *Synonym:* Home Health Agency (HHA); Home Care Program; within a hospital organization it may be called the Home Care Department.

Hospital Satellite—a geographically freestanding facility which is owned, governed, or managed by a hospital or an independent entity. Different types include: (1) hospital sponsored, (2) hospital association, (3) independent operation.

Joint Planning—two or more health care providers planning on a project or program to meet the health care requirements of their respective localities. Planning could be either clinical or administrative in nature.

Joint Purchasing Agreement—a formal agreement among two or more health providers, facilities, or programs to purchase services and/or goods (e.g. equipment or supplies). The agreements simplify purchasing and result in economies of scale. The intent is to lower costs to the institutions.

Joint Venture—an organization or association formed by two or more parties usually formed for a single purpose or undertaking. Such organizations may make its membership liable for the organization's debts.

Limited Partnership—a certain type of partnership which limits the liability of certain partners (inactive) to their investment in the enterprise only. At least one member of the partnership must be fully responsible for all debts.

Long-Term Care—health, medical, and social services provided on a continual basis to patients suffering from chronic medical and mental conditions.

Magnetic Resonance Imaging (MRI)—a diagnostic procedure that produces tomographic images. This procedure requires specialized equipment consisting of large magnets and radio signals. The result is images of the patient's anatomical structures. The diagnostic tool also has the capability of evaluating a patient's chemical disturbances at the cellular level. The old term for this was Nuclear Magnetic Resonance (NMR).

Marketing Audit—a marketing tool which provides an extensive view of a hospital's or a business's services; it provides a perspective of the services' image and the market segments.

Marketing Plan/Program—the process of presenting services/products to the marketplace. It involves product definition; product location or place; the price of the product to the consumer/customer, and the promotion of the product, including public relations and advertising.

Market Research—the planning for, obtaining, displaying, and analyzing data related to the marketing of a product/service.

Medical Office Building (MOB)—a freestanding building or a structure attached to a hospital or a floor of the hospital where a physician or health practitioner can establish an office. An MOB may be a marketing tool for a hospital to attract and retain physicians.

Merger—the resulting condition after one business or corporation secures the capital stock of another business. The merged corporation stock is usually then dissolved.

MeSH—a particular type of corporation as a result of joint venture between hospitals and physicians. It is a form of partnership. This type of organization allows hospitals and physicians to more readily and appropriately respond to the changes in the health care system.

Multihospital System—a central association that owns, leases, and controls, by contract, two or more hospitals. Some of the benefits of such a system are: easier availability of capital markets, mutual purchasing for greater economies of scale, and mutual use of technical and management personnel. There are two types of multihospital systems, either not-for-profit (which includes church-affiliated) and investor-owned (for profit). *Synonym:* Multis.

Multi-Institutional Arrangement—two or more organizations structured in a specific way or for a special purpose.

Partnership—a legal form of business organization. It consists of two or more individuals with each individual assuming full personal liability for the debts of the business. *Synonym:* General Partnership.

Perspective Payment System (PPS)—a method of payment to hospitals whereby a rate is established for a service in advance (e.g., the federal government's PPS).

Preferred Provider Organization (PPO)—an assortment of direct contractual arrangements among hospitals, physicians, insurers, employers, or third-party administrators in which providers join together to offer health care for a distinct group of people, and which normally have three distinguishing features in common: (1) discounts from standard charges (2) monetary goals for single subscribers (insureds) to utilize contracting providers, and (3) broad utilization review programs.

Primary Care Center—an organization offering primary care on a fixed schedule and available around eight hours daily. The staff is composed of either a physician assistant or a primary care physician and is upheld by standard laboratory and often radiology services. Follow-up care is usually offered.

Public Relations—a two-way communication bridge to a relationship with the public, employees, and a vehicle to support fund raising; a tool in consumer action.

Shared Services—clinical or administrative services offered by two or more hospitals in a joint arrangement for their mutual benefit (e.g. a centralized data processing system or a cooperative organ transplantation program are two examples of shared services.

Shared Services Organization—a separate legal entity established by two or more organizations or institutions that allows for joint control by the sponsoring organizations or institutions.

Subsidiary—a company controlled by a "parent organization" which owns all or most of the subsidiary's shares. Although the subsidiary supports the parent company financially, they do not always engage in the same line of business.

Tax Equity and Fiscal Responsibility Act of 1982 (TEFRA)—P.L. 97-248 which covers many far reaching Medicare amendments as applied to hospital reimbursement policies. This law was a first step in placing hospitals on a prospective pricing system (PPS) rather than the retrospective cost system.

Tax Exempt Revenue Bonds—a source of debt financing with two major features: (1) the interest received by bond holders is not subject to federal income tax; (2) the organization receiving the financing secures the bonds with its gross revenues.

Teaching Hospital—a hospital that provides undergraduate or graduate medical education, usually with one or more medical, dental internship and/or residency programs in affiliation with a medical school.

Urgent Care Center—a freestanding facility which provides minor emergency (nonlife threatening) care, or basic health services on a nonscheduled basis. *Synonyms:* Urgicenter; "Doc in the Box," Freestanding Emergency Room, Walk in Clinic.

Venture Capital—capital funds subject to considerable risk which are generally used in the development of new business activities. *Synonym:* Risk Capital.

Voluntary Hospitals of America (VHA)—a nationwide alliance of 450 private not-for-profit hospitals which came together in order to derive benefits similar to those of centrally managed chains, while maintaining their local ownership and autonomy. Formed in 1977 and based in Irving, Texas, the alliance offers members services such as group purchasing and management services. It is now setting up an HMO/PPO joint venture with a large health insurer. VHA's mission is to preserve and promote the "stand-alone" health care institution in an age of increased competition from "chains."

Wellness—the concept of an individual having or striving for a positive state of health. It involves the physical, mental, and emotional elements.

Appendix I

Selected Annotated Bibliography

KEY RESOURCE DOCUMENTS

Health Care Joint Ventures: Survey Results. New York: Ernst and Whitney, 1985. (86pp.) A survey of 400 hospitals formed the basis for this overview of "what's hot and what's not" in joint venture activity. Commentary on trends in planning and implementing joint ventures is substantiated with detailed survey results.

"Joint Ventures in Health Care," Valentine, S.T. (ed.) *Topics in Health Care Financing* 12(2) (Winter 1985). (85pp.) An initial reference source which provides comprehensive coverage of basic concepts. Experts in the field contributed chapters on evaluating opportunities, financing, pricing/reimbursement, marketing, organizational structure, tax advantages, securities placement. Several case studies illustrate principles.

HOSPITAL-PHYSICIAN JOINT VENTURES

"Ambulatory Care Joint Ventures Rise." *Hospitals* 60(3) (February 1986): 59. A recent survey by this publication showed that the larger the hospital, the more likely it was to be involved in a joint venture. Closer ties with medical staff and increased referrals were the reasons given most frequently as rationales for initiating these kinds of arrangements. Ambulatory surgery centers were the most prevalent ventures.

"An Alliance in Medical Field Forged Out of Fear," Gaul, G.M. *The Philadelphia Inquirer* (May 25, 1986):F-3, 13. Examples of recent hospital-physician business alliances in Philadelphia are attributed to fear of losing their traditional market share. Physicians assert that their

---

Note: The Selected Annotated Bibliography was prepared by Kathleen M. Ahrens, MS, Director of Information Services, Presbyterian-University of Pennsylvania Medical Center.

primary motivation in these ventures is not profit, but concern for quality of care.

"Are Hospitals and Physicians Allies or Rivals in Ambulatory Care?" Burns, L.A. *Trustee* 36(7)(July 1983):26–28, 31–32. Strategies for board members to ease tensions and promote cooperation between the hospital and its medical staff through joint ventures in ambulatory care.

"Avoiding Problems in Hospital-Physician Joint Ventures," Goldblatt, S.J. *Healthcare Financial Management* 38(2)(February 1984):88–90, 92. Hospitals now view Physicians Office Buildings (POBs) as traditional real estate ventures with the dual purpose of attracting physicians and patients as well as acting as a barrier against competitors. Relationships with POB partners who are physicians must be structured carefully to protect all of the parties involved.

"Cooperation between Hospitals and Physicians for Better Cost-Effective Medical Care Delivery—The Health Care Joint Venture." Couch, J.B. and Caesar, N.B. *Philadelphia Medicine* 81(12)(December 1985):534–8. The authors advise hospitals and physicians to heed the pharmacological principles of synergism: the combined positive effect of two diverse agents may be greater that the sum of their individual parts.

"Finding the Shoe That Fits," Carpenter, R.B. *Hospital Forum* 1984 27(5)(September/October 1984):14–8. This article examines different ways in which hospitals and their medical staffs can seek opportunities in the marketplace of PPOs, HMOs, and other potential joint ventures in both the DRG and capitation sides of Medicare.

"Going into Business Together: Whether We Like It or Not," Spence, M. *Healthcare Executive* 1(2)(February 1986):16–20. The author, a physician, advises hospitals to build sound business relationships with only the best and brightest—not all—of its medical staff. The how-to's for creating these joint ventures are outlined.

"Guide to Developing and Operating an Ambulatory Care Center," Manson, L. *Hospital Forum* 27(5)(September–October 1984):21–25. Misunderstandings about control/management can cause as much tension as allocation of profits in a joint venture. The ambulatory center described was designed with special attention to the delineation of responsibilities and powers.

"Hospital-Physician MRI Joint Ventures," Braun, P. *Administrative Radiology* pp. 23–5. Radiologists and hospital administrators—accustomed to relating to each other at arms-length—are now collaborating to share the risk and cost ($3 million plus) of this new technology.

"Hospital-Physician Joint Ventures," Paris, M. *Hospital Management: Winning Strategies for the '80s* (J. Peña et al, eds.), Rockville: MD: Aspen Publishers, 1985. This is a comprehensive review of hospital-physician joint ventures including historical perspectives, examples, structures, rationales, negotiation strategies, and implications for the future.

"Hospital-Physician Joint Ventures: Some Crucial Considerations." Mancino, D.M. *Hospital Progress* 65(1)(January 1984):30–5. Before entering a joint venture the hospital should prioritize its objectives, structure the relationship with partners and select an appropriate investment vehicle.

"Hospital-Physician Joint Ventures: Who's Doint What" Morrisey, M.A. and Brooks, D.C. *Hospitals* 59(9)(May 1985):74, 76, 78. A 1984 American Hospital Association survey showed that hospital-physician joint ventures were still in infancy, with fewer that 12 percent of hospitals reporting such arrangements.

"Hospital-Staff Ventures Popular, But Critics Question Their Worth." Richman, D. *Modern Healthcare* 15(11)(May 1985):80–1. Critics charge that through joint ventures hospitals are losing the advantage the physician surplus has created for them and that they should be hiring physicians as employees not preserving the private practice system.

"Hospitals, Physicians Seeking Ventures with Surgery Centers." Wallace, C. *Modern Healthcare* 3;60(1)(January 1986):70. The surgery center industry is beginning to consolidate and review its business practices as pending legislation to lower hospital outpatient surgery rates encourages hospitals and physicians to look for outside alliances.

"Hospitals Share Financing Risks, Gain Marketing Advantages with Joint Venture Partners," Maier, R. *Linc Letter* 1(3)(June 1985):1–2. Benefits for physician-partners are reviewed.

"Hospitals Tap Group Practices Most Often for Joint Ventures." *Medical Staff News* (October 1985), p. 4. Excerpts from the Ernst & Whinney survey demonstrate that physician practice groups are hospitals' most common partners in ambulatory care and alternative delivery systems.

"How Do Joint Ventures Affect Relations with Physicians?" Richards, G. *Hospitals* 58(23)(December 1984):68, 70, 72. Members of the Baylor Physicians Associates claim that joint ventures improved the cohesiveness of their group and provided a legal vehicle for dealing with the hospital.

"Joint Adventures in the Healthcare Jungle," Thompson, R.E. *Healthcare Executive* 1(2)(February 1986):24–27. Six keys to success for hospital executives from a physician investor, including how to educate and approach members of the medical staff without making them feel like just "deep pockets."

"Joint Venture Savvy." *Hospital Medical Staff* 13(10)(October 1984):29. When selecting a joint venture partner, physicians are cautioned to ask not only "what's in it for me?", but also what's in the deal for the patients.

"Joint Ventures: The Trends and the Potential Pitfalls," Wolff, S.O. *Trustee* 38(10)(October 1985):13–16. A review of critical factors affecting the success or failure of hospital-physician joint ventures such as objective analysis of partners' motives, the necessity of feasibility studies, etc.

"Joint Ventures in Ambulatory Care," Bermas, N.F. *Journal of Ambulatory Care Management* 8(4)(November 1985):79–87. Various forms of ambulatory care joint ventures are described including medical office buildings, primary care centers, ambulatory surgery centers, and other specialized diagnostic and treatment services.

"Joint Venturing Your Outpatient Cardiac Cath Lab." *Hospital Entrepreneurs' Newsletter* 1(7)(December 1985):3,6–8. Facts and figures are presented to show how hospitals and their cardiologists can "package" their cardiac cath lab with other procedures to provide an edge in negotiating with HMOs and PPOs.

"Market Forces Set Off Skyrocketing Interest in Hospital-Doctor Ventures," Rosenfield, R.H. *Modern Healthcare* 14(6)(May 1984):70,72,74. Contractual, corporate, and limited partnership models are reviewed as viable structures for hospital-doctor joint ventures.

"Meet Your New Business Partner-The Hospital," Hunt, K. *Medical Economics* 15(October 1984) pp. 87–88,91–92,94. Information for the physician emphasizing the "what's in it for you?" aspects of joint ventures with hospitals.

"Partnership Allows High-Tech Purchase." *Hospitals.* 57(19)(October 1983):33,36. To acquire digital subtraction angiography equipment, a hospital formed a limited partnership between its for-profit affiliate and local physicians. The benefits include tax advantages and more efficient operation.

"Pioneer Partnership of Physicians, Hospitals." *Medical World News* 26(19)(October 1985):156. The Robert Wood Johnson Foundation's eight-year Community Hospital Program to establish outpatient clinics is reviewed.

"Physicians, Rochester, NY, Hospital Enter Joint Venture to Protect Market," Tatge, M. *Modern Healthcare* 14(16)(December 1984):26. In a city where there were already four HMOs, physicians at Highland Hospital formed a MeSH partnership to start their own health plan.

"Surgicenter Joint Venture Development," Montrose, G.D. *Hospital Entrepreneurs' Newsletter* 1(11)(April 1986):1–5. The growth of surgicenters was thought to have peaked in 1984, when proprietary corporations dominated the market. Today, most of these corporations are selling off their unprofitable centers and are pursuing joint ventures and management contracts with already successful surgicenters.

"The Physician as a Source of Hospital Capital," Fried, J.M. *Hospital Progress* 65(6)(June 1984):54–6. As hospitals search for means of financing renovation during the next decade, physicians will represent a source of capital through tax-shelter financing.

"Ventures Show Cooperation with MDs Up." *Hospitals* 59(19)(October 1985):37–40. Highlights of the Ernst & Whiney Survey emphasizing market-oriented reasons for hospital-physician relationships. Article includes "five ways to kill a joint venture" and go/no go checklist.

PARTNERS OTHER THAN PHYSICIANS

"Affiliations with Multis: Rurals Becoming Picky." Powills, S. *Hospitals* 59(17)(September 1985):412. Although it is no longer a seller's market for small and rural hospitals, some are aggressively seeking affiliation with multis.

"AMI, St. Luke's Episcopal Discussing Integrated Delivery System for Houston." Wallace, C. *Modern Healthcare* 15(4)(February 1985):135. Networking is believed to be the survival strategy of the future. Elements of a good network include primary, secondary, and tertiary care; good geographical distribution of health services; and marketing of health insurance products to individuals and groups.

"Blue Cross President Sees Joint Ventures as Objective Delivery/Financing Linkage." *FAH Review* 19(1)(January–February 1986):39–40. Bernard Tresnowki, CEO of BX/BS, views joint ventures as the ideal structure for cooperation between delivery and financing so that linking parties can maintain their respective business objectives and conflicting interests don't compromise the current situation in healthcare.

"Catholics Consolidate: Roman Catholic Systems Move Toward Affiliations and Mergers." Grayson, M.A. *Multis* 2(5)(October 1985):M9–M13. According to CHA the number of Catholic multi-institutional arrangements have almost doubled between 1979 and 1985.

"Chains Cool to Teaching Centers." *Medical World News* 27(3)(February 1986):35. Bleak earnings are forecast for early attempts at joint ventures between for-profit chains and academic health centers.

"Diverse Partners Join Hospitals in Ventures." Richman, D. *Modern Healthcare* 15(11)(May 1985):75–6. Some new innovations include a "risk capital pool" for funding profitable ideas to support worthwhile hospital programs that regularly lose money; a collaboration between two large multi's to develop a chain of industrial medical clinics and independent clinical laboratories seeking arrangements with hospitals ranging from management contracts to full partnerships.

"Hahnemann Plans Second Campus." Gaul, G.M. *Philadelphia Inquirer* (June 1986):11-D. An agreement between a medical school and a suburban multi-hospital system will provide clinical training sites for students and build a strong university-related residency program for the community hospitals. The partners are also exploring other joint efforts such as an HMO.

"HCMR Interviews Executives in a Shared-Service Joint Venture." *Health*

Care Management Review 10(2)(Spring 1985):85–93. This home health care joint venture between ServiceMaster and three hospitals illustrates the new kinds of relationships developing as the health care industry moves to a more market-oriented system.

"Home Healthcare Service Company Forges Joint Ventures with Hospitals," Wallace, C. *Modern Healthcare* 16(2)(January 1986):50. Several hospitals and a California home health service company have formed profitable joint ventures in the home infusion therapy market.

"Hospitals Form Joint Ventures with For-profit Corporations To Develop Freestanding Surgery Centers." *Outreach* 6(5)(September–October 1985):1. Companies whose main business is the development of FSCs are affiliating with hospitals that can provide space and are willing to share the risks as well as profits.

"Joint Arrrangements between Hospitals and Long-Term Care Facilities," Wood, Lucksinger, and Epstein. *Health Law Outlook* 5(1)(January 1986):1–4. Hosptials responding to PPS are entering into bed reserve agreements to assure their patients places in long-term care facilities. Several legal considerations are discussed, including tax exempt/for-profit ventures, management contracts, federal tax implications, fraud/abuse, and other issues.

"Joint Venture Fever Hits Air Force, VA." *Hospitals* 60(13)(July 1986):114. Two government agencies, the Air Force and Veterans Administration, have mirrored their civilian counterparts by forming a joint venture to lease and construct new hospitals. Lower costs and expanded beneficiary services are cited as reasons for the arrangement.

"Joint Ventures for MRI's Create Regulatory Grey Areas" *Hospitals* 59(16)(August 1985):100, 105. Medicare payment can be made only to recognized provider categories such as hospitals or physicians. Joint venture diagnostic centers have not been given a "pigeonhole" by HCFA.

"Joint Ventures with Industry May Solve the Shortage of Educational Funds." Thompson, R.E. *Modern Healthcare* 15(14)(July 1985):224. The new "facts of life" for financing medical education are reviewed. The author calls for new arrangements that would involve industry in philanthropic partnerships in medical education similar to those existing in other cultural and educational events.

"Life Insurers in Joint Venture with Hospitals," Haggerty, A.G. *National Underwriter (Life Health)* 90(3)(January 1986). Two insurers, Transamerica Occidental Life and Provident Life and Casualty linked up with American Healthcare Systems' 1300 hospitals to form PPOs and HMOs in 48 states.

"McDonnell Douglas, Insurer Start Joint Venture," Kastiel, D.L. *Business Insurance* 19(46)(November 1985):26. A Fortune 500 aerospace company and a large life/health insurer have teamed up to offer health insurance products, including an HMO and PPO to St. Louis-area employers.

"Marketing Impact of a Joint Venture: Can Home Health Agencies Meet the Challenge?" Jay, T. and Logsdon, J. *Caring* 4(9)(September 1985):42–5. When the two major hospitals in Schenectady started their own home care services, the existing Visiting Nurses Association decided not to fight them, but to join them. The partners were able to offer a wider spectrum of hi-tech services to the community and collaborated on planning, marketing, and training.

"More Hospitals Will Use Joint Ventures To Enter Home Care Market-Experts." Anderson, H.J. *Modern Healthcare* 15(23)(November, 1985):51–2. Hospitals will continue to enter the home care market, but many will do so through joint ventures with chains or cooperative arrangements with existing agencies rather than go it alone.

"MRI Paints Bright Picture for Imaging Center Partnerships." Johnson, D.E.L. *Modern Healthcare* 14(6)(May 1984):61–2,68. Industry experts predict that two thousand imaging centers will open in the next five years. Hospitals will act as general partners with physicians and will venture with outside developers. The advantages of freestanding centers are stressed.

"Multis and Teaching Hospitals." Douglass, R. *Multis* 2(4)(August 1985): M23–4, M28–9. In the last year, at least eight teaching hospitals or research facilities reached contractual agreements with investor-owned multis. Since proprietary systems are generally more community oriented, it remains to be seen whether they can meet the unique needs of teaching hospitals.

"Oklahoma System is Goal of Venture." *Modern Healthcare* 15(10)(May 1985):22. A new for-profit company plans to build a statewide network of acute, psychiatric, and long-term care facilities. This will provide a "presence" in Oklahoma for the California-based partner and a strong financial partner for a well-known Catholic teaching hospital.

"Philly Hospitals Join in Shared Research Project." *Hospitals* 60(10)(May 1986):62,64. Twenty-four Philadelphia-area hospitals jointly commissioned a market research project that provided data for strategic planning and a significant savings in consultants fees. The partners each received individualized reports, after they had collectively devised a 77-item questionnaire that was used to conduct 6,000 telephone interviews.

"Physical Therapy: A Venture Toward Success." *Optimal Health* (May–June 1986):72–7. Two Chicago hospitals join forces with a health club in a physical therapy venture that promises lower costs, higher profits, and a built-in patient base.

"Pittsburgh Area is Home of Largest MRI Joint Venture." *Hospitals*

59(16)(August 1985):106. Environmental factors, such as the resources to become a national MRI research and development center and a waning local economy, provided the impetus for 12 local hospitals and Carnegie Mellon University to form this not-for-profit corporation.

"Provider Case Studies Highlight Joint Activities in Long-Term Care." Pulling, M.O. *Healthcare Financial Management* 39(8):78,80,82,84. Joint activities between community acute care hospitals and long-term care facilities are increasing as hospitals learn how to control "vertical integration" using a variety of corporate structures and diversification strategies.

"Public Health Deficits Spur Hospital Joint Ventures." *Hospitals* 59(10) (May 1985):70. As federal budget cuts affect public health agencies, home health ventures among hospitals are becoming popular arrangements.

"Safety of Joint Ventures May Attract Hospitals." Mistarz, J.E. *Hospitals* 58(5)(March 1984):42,44. Examples of various "menus" of home health services offered by independent companies as part of joint ventures with hospitals are reviewed.

"Teaching-Hospital Links with For-Profits Up: Study." *Hospitals* 59(22) (November 1985):26. Five of 23 for-profit chains surveyed indicated an interest in linking with an academic health center.

"VHA Hoping Deals Will Create Its 'Brand' of National Healthcare," Barkholz, D. *Modern Healthcare* 15(14)(July 1985):82. This chain of 450 not-for-profit hospitals formed a preferred provider organization and health maintenance organization joint venture with an insurance company, Aetna Life & Casualty, expecting to attract 5 million enrollees in 3–5 years.

"VHA Plans Joint Venture with Suppliers to Make Package Products for Members." *Modern Healthcare* 15(7)(March 1986):60. In 1984, Voluntary Hospitals of America (VHA) joined with pharmaceutical companies to lower the cost of drugs and supplies to its 411 member hospitals. Future venture partners will allow VHA to expand its product line to include hospital forms, bandages and orthopedic softgoods, as well as other supply items.

"Zayre Ventures into Healthcare Facilities," Moran, S.E. *Advertising Age* 57(43)(August 1986):22. Two Chicago-area Zayre stores will have satellite clinics of Mount Sinai Hospital tucked in among their racks of running shoes and laundry detergent. The clinics, called "Family Health Corner," will specialize in physical examinations, routine dentistry, and podiatry.

MARKETING

"Assign Marketing to Skilled Partner." Franz, J. *Modern Healthcare* 14(7) (May 1984):76. Whether marketing should be done by the hospital, physicians' group, or an outside agency, is a point of contention in joint ventures. This article explains how the strengths of each group can be synthesized into a viable marketing program.

"Collecting Marketing Research Data." Dickson, J.P. and Dickson, S.S. *Nonprofit World Report* 3(2)(March–April 1985):19–21,29. Techniques for choosing a survey method, designing the form, sampling the constituency, and collecting the data are discussed.

"Focus Groups: Assessing Patient Satisfaction and Targeting New Services." DeWolf, L. *Hospital Topics* 63(2)(March–April 1985):24–6. Taking their cue from business and industry, some hospitals have found focus groups to be an effective way to interactively communicate with consumers. Guidelines for conducting a productive group encounter are presented.

"Guidelines: Advertising by Hospitals." American Hospital Association (1977):1–2. This document was approved by the AHA General Council in 1984 and is intended to provide general advice to the membership.

"The Health Care Market Audit." Macstravic, R.E. *Health Progress* 59(10) (October 1978):63–5, 90. Reviews the market audit processes of identifying, collecting, and evaluating information.

"The Importance of Marketing Research to the Nonprofit Organization." Dickson, J.P. and Dickson, S.S. *Nonprofit World Report* 2(6)(November–December 1984):12–14. Basic questions and useful answers about the nature of marketing research and its use by nonprofit planners.

"The Market for Health Services: Is There a Nontraditional Consumer?" Berkowitz, E.N. and Flexner, W. *Journal of Health Care Marketing* 1(1)(Winter 1980–1981):25–34. This early marketing study answered the question "Who is really the consumer in health care?" Researchers documented a shift in decision making from physician to patients. Health delivery planners were advised to monitor this "transitional" segment of the new, more proactive consumer market.

"Marketing-A Tool for Survival." Herkimer A.G. *Healthcare Financial Management* 34(9)(September 1980):12–3, 16, 18. Elucidates the role of the Chief Financial Officer in the health care institution's marketing effort.

"Marketing Ambulatory Care to Women: A Segmentation Approach." Harrell, G.C. and Fors, M.F. *Journal of Health Care Marketing* 5(2)

(Spring 1985):19–28. The authors contend that most market research is generated by treatment-based needs and focuses too often on general public as consumers. They propose exploratory study of population segments—in this case, five categories of female health consumers—as the first step in target marketing.

"Marketing Assures a Satellite Facility a Safe Send-Off." McLaren, J.A. and Traeger, B.S. *Hospitals* 51(11)(June 1977):67–9. Marketing, development, and public relations functions were combined to carefully design and promote a joint venture between a hospital and a church.

"The Marketing Audit: A Tool for Health Service Organizations." Berkowitz, E.N. and Flexner, W.A. *Health Care Management Review* 3(4)(Fall 1978):51–57. Practical information on how to develop and implement a marketing plan is given and summarized in a checklist of questions to be answered during the audit.

"Marketing Traps: 13 Tips on How Not To Proceed." Martin, L.Z. *Hospital Forum* 4(4)(March–April 1985):27–8. Marketing is the process of giving people what they want, not attempting to make people want what the hospital has to sell.

"Professional May be Held to Higher Advertising Standards, Court Rules." Horty, J.F. *Modern Healthcare* 11(10)(September 1981):112–5. Recent court rulings indicate that advertising by professionals will be held to a very high standard of accuracy and completeness.

"Questionnaires Determine Patient Satisfaction." Jessee, W.F. *Hospital Peer Review* 6(5)(May 1981):53–5. Patient questionnaires provide feedback on the institution's "caring" functions as well as its "curing" abilities. A sample questionnaire is included.

"Surveys Can Provide Good Feedback." *Hospitals* 54(14)(July 1980):14. Two suggestions for effective patient survey questions are "What are two things about our hospital that you would change?" and "Name an employee who deserves special recognition."

"The Telemarketing Industry: Where We Are—Where We're Going." Lison, C. *Telemarketing* 4(1)(July 1985):22–27, 59, 67–8. A survey of telemarketers across the country provided this state-of-the-art overview. Continued growth of telemarketing as "the primary sales approach" is predicted.

"10 Reasons Hospital Marketing Programs Fail." Hauser, L.J. *Hospitals* 58(17)(September 1984):74–7. Pitfalls including problems with physicians, trustees, lack of commitment or investment capital, confusing marketing with sales or advertising, and other critical factors are described.

PLANNING, ORGANIZATION, AND CONTROL

"Alta Bates' Subsidiary Mulls Network of MRI Centers in San Francisco Area." Wallace, C. *Modern Healthcare* 15(19)(September 1985):76. The new for-profit subsidiary of this California-based multihospital system is establishing a network of magnetic resonance imaging (MRI) centers in the San Francisco area in an effort to package an attractive product for insurers and prepaid plans. Joint venture partners include other hospitals' and physicians' groups.

"Beyond the Reagan Tax Proposal: Hospital Capital Management Strategies." Harris, J.P. *Healthcare Financial Management* 39(11)(November 1985);80–2,84. If Reagan's tax proposal is implemented, low-cost tax-exempt revenue bonds, advance refunding, and the investment tax credit would be eliminated. Such possibilities could cause a serious blow to the hospital industry—the cost of capital could rise significantly, the hospital's ability to manage debt could decrease, and joint ventures could become less attractive.

"Break-Even Analysis Gives Manager Flexibility and Control in Making Decisions." Snook, I.D., Jr. *Healthcare Financial Management* 29(9)(September 1975):58–60, 62. From the administrator's point of view, being able to determine when the revenue from patient services will exactly equal operating expenses is critical to managing the hospital.

"Charting the Course of Your Institution's Joint Venture." Sandrick, K. *Trustee* 38(10)(October 1985):17–9. Board members are advised to establish a favorable milieu for joint venturing and, using their experience as leaders of business, to act as financial advisors to the hospital and its partners.

"Competition for Healthcare Markets Spurs Race for Demographic Data." White, E.C. *Modern Healthcare* 15(20)(September 1985):79–80, 82. Several new demographic data products have been developed to aid health care planners in their quest for market intelligence.

"Fighting Off Competition by a Joint Venture in Outpatient Surgery." Holl, E.F. *Topics in Health Care Financing* 12(2)(Winter 1985);58–65. A case study of a hypothetic joint venture between a hospital and its medical staff is presented. Data for the business plan and marketing strategies are introduced.

"HHS Begins To Monitor Recent Joint Ventures." Sax, B.M. *Hospitals* 59(21)(November 1985);87,90. As business relationships in health care become more creative and sophisticated, the industry moves closer to conflict with the U.S. Department of Health and Human Services statutes prohibiting remuneration for referrals.

"Hospital Diversification Strategies: Lessons from Other Industries." Coddington, D.C. and Pottle, J.T. *Healthcare Financial Management* 38(12)(December 1984):19–20,24. Drawing from successful and unsuccessful business strategies in broadcasting and defense—two industries that had to diversify in order to survive—hospitals are advised to develop economic feasibility criteria for screening potential ventures, to stay close to familiar lines of business, to have reasonable time/profit expectations, and to expect some failures and unanticipated capital expenses.

"Hospital Revenue Diversification: A Case Study in Joint Venture Investing." Gilbert, R.N. *Healthcare Financial Management* 40(4)(April 1986): 46–50. The subject of this case study is a 350-bed community hospital that diversified into diagnostic imaging, outpatient surgery, and urgent care centers, as well as consulting businesses in hospital telecommunications and data processing. Lessons learned include using a separate project management team, cultivating support from the right board members, obtaining commitments for 150% of the estimated funding, and incorporating escape clauses in partnerships.

"Hospitals Turning to Joint Ventures to Gain Access to Costly Equipment." Jackson, G. and Jensen, J. *Modern Healthcare* 14(10)(October 1984):108–10. This survey showed that 4 out of 10 hospitals nationwide are either currently joint venturing or planning to enter arrangements with partners to acquire equipment. Partners included other hospitals, corporations, individuals, and physicians.

"Joint Ventures in Health Care: What To Do before You Do the Deal." Kaufman, K.; Hall, M.; and Higgins, D. *Healthcare Financial Management* 40(7)(July 1986):66–7,70–4. This article focuses on evaluation, structuring, and implementation strategies for joint ventures. These functions give the venture direction, provide better understanding of the transaction, and create an overall businesslike attitude.

"Joint Ventures Revisited: We're All in This Together." Kaufman, K., Hall, M., and Higgins, D. *Healthcare Financial Management* 40(10)(March 1986):108–10. Three models for structuring joint ventures are described.

"Joint Ventures: the Theory and Practice." Swett, T.F. and Conley, D.J. *Hospitals* 58(7)(May 1984):95–6,99–100. This detailed analysis of a hypothetical joint venture explains the advantages to both hospitals and investors.

"Joint Venturing Can Lead to Insurance Problems." *PHICO Forum* (March 1986). Hospitals should consult their insurance carriers before finalizing joint venture plans. Some coverages for environmental, product, or Director's/Officer's liability for new firms are very difficult to obtain.

"Mergers, Acquisitions and Affiliations," Kepner, J.C.S. *Series Health Law Newsletter* (Saul, Ewing, Remick, & Saul); July 1986. This is a 21-item checklist to use in evaluating cooperative ventures among health care facilities.

"Nine Pitfalls for the Unwary." Jones, W.J. *Hospital Forum* 27(5)(September–October 1984):50–1. Common mistakes health care executives make when they are facing their first joint ventures with physicians.

"Rate of Return: A Tool to Evaluate Diversification." Harris, J. and Ruetz, J. *Healthcare Financial Management* 38(12)(December 1984):28–32, 34. The potential risks and returns of various diversification opportunities can be projected using required, risk adjusted, and expected internal rate of return (IRR) models.

"Reserving Nursing Home Beds: Evaluating the Feasibility for the Hospital and the Long-Term Care Facility. Part 1: Do They Make Economic Sense?" *Healthcare Financial Management* 40(2)(February 1986):34, 36–40. Before entering into a bed reserve agreement, a hospital and nursing home must carefully examine the economic considerations—cost, revenue, and price—which benefit each partner.

"Selling Your Concept: How to Prepare and Market an Effective Business Plan." Harris, J.P. *Topics in Health Care Financing* 12(2)(Winter 1985):32–7. The mechanics of writing a plan and suggestions for its presentation are reviewed.

"Strategies for Survival in the Hospital Industry." Coddington, D.C., Palmquist, L.E., and Trollinger, W.V. *Harvard Business Review* 63(3)(May–June 1985):129–38. The advantages and disadvantages of downsizing, diversification, and joint ventures have to be weighed by hospitals if they are to maintain both good levels of care and a sound financial base.

"Watch Out for Surgicenter Joint Venture Pitfalls." *Hospitals* 60(14)(July 1986):46. Jealousy among physicians, sponsorship of freestanding centers by anesthesiologists, and a cavalier attitude toward competition, are a few of problems that surgicenter ventures have encountered.

LEGAL CONSIDERATIONS

"Antitrust, Joint Ventures and the End of the AMA's Contract Practice Ethics: New Ways of Thinking about the Health Care Industry." Weller, C.D. *Specialty Law Digest Health Care* 6(8)(October 1984):7–36. Large groups, such as the AMA, can no longer join together to take economic action within the health care delivery system. This author contends that the "era of guild ethics is over" and that the present legal climate favors small groups of competitors.

"Canonical Considerations in Corporate Restructuring." Holland, S. *Health Progress* 66(2)(March 1985):36–9,46. Under the Catholic Church's Code of Canon Law, civil documents, such as agreements for entering joint ventures, must include provisions that preserve the Catholic partner's religious identity and protect the Church's assets.

"Hospitals' Joint Ventures, Incentive Plans May Violate Fraud, Abuse Laws." Wallace, C. *Modern Healthcare* 15(1)(January 1985):23–4. A gray area exists where there is little federal guidance on fraud and abuse laws relating to health care ventures. The legality of new methods of attracting patients, such as waiving fees to attract Medicare clients, is questionable.

"Joint Venture Structures: The Right Choice." Silbermann, B.D. *Healthcare Executive* 1(3)(March–April 1986):38–40. Physicians and hospitals are scrambling to not only seek positive joint venture relationships, but to directly tie quality with economic control of patient care. PPOs, public and private placement, limited partnerships, and hospital ownership by physicians are reviewed.

"Joint Ventures and Illegal Remuneration: The Pressure is Growing." Sax, B.M. *Healthcare Financial Management* 40(3)(March 1986):398–41. An attorney reviews court decisions related to the soliciting, receiving, offering, or paying of remuneration in return for the referral of patients or generation of business.

"Joint Ventures in Health Care: More Than a Sideline Business." Kaufman, K.; Hall, M. and Higgins, D. *Healthcare Financial Management* 40(5)(May 1986):68–72,74. Health care joint ventures are sometimes considered second class businesses. However, compared to other small enterprises, health care ventures present an array of unique and complex issues such as organizational form, antitrust, reimbursement, licensing, and securities laws that must be understood and resolved.

"Joint Ventures: Legal Issues in New Forms of Hospital-Physician Relationships." *Health Law Update* 1(3)(Fall 1985):2,6–7. Ten legal issues and problems inherent in creating new organizational and operational structures that link hospitals and physicians are reviewed.

"Medicare and Medicaid-Sanctions for Fraud and Abuse: A Key Consideration in Structuring Joint Ventures." *Health Law Update* 1(2)(Spring 1985):1,8. A prime rule in avoiding violations of fraud and abuse regulations is to emphasize services and contributions that are not tied to rewards for referrals or purchases of goods and services. Examples of compliance and noncompliance are presented.

"Not-For-Profits Must Eye Tax Status." *Modern Healthcare* 15(11)(May 1985):76. The authors suggest that hospitals obtain a favorable letter ruling from IRS before entering into a joint venture.

"Participation in Joint Ventures, PPOs and IPAs May Threaten Pension Plans." Peters, G. *Healthcare Financial Management* 38(10)(October 1984):68–70, 72. The federal tax qualification under Internal Revenue Code Section 414(m) regarding employee benefit plans may be jeopardized as hospitals, physicians, and physician professional corporations enter into joint ventures. The author reviews structures that may provide some relief from the 414(m) dilemma.

"Practical Guide to Health Care Antitrust Issues." Kopit, W.G.; Barnes, C.E.; and Latorre, L. *Trustee* 39(5)(May 1986):16. To reduce the hospital's antitrust liability in joint activities, the enterprise must not be achievable by the individual partners and must not restrict entry of other competitors into the market.

"Public Hospitals: The Legal Obstacles of Entering into Joint Ventures." Miller, J.N. *Healthcare Financial Management* 40(3)(March 1986):44–48. Special considerations are involved in joint venturing with public hospitals. However, this attorney maintains that, with a little creativity and preseverance, public hospitals can compete in the joint venture arena.

"Reserving Nursing Home Beds: Evaluating the Feasibility for the Hospital and the Long-Term Care Facility. Part 2: Are They a Legal Alternative?" *Healthcare Financial Management* 40(2)(February 1986):35,42–6. Although carefully structured bed reserve agreements will be sanctioned by HCFA, acute and long-term care partners are advised to seek legal counsel to verify that their particular type of arrangement is acceptable.

"Tax-Exempt Hospitals and Joint Ventures: Does One Jeopardize the Other?" Mancino, D.M. *Healthcare Financial Management* 39(9)(September 1985):68–70,72,74. A tax attorney enumerates the pitfalls that can cause a hospital to lose its tax-exempt status.

Index

V

W

About the Authors

I. DONALD SNOOK, JR. is a nationally renowned leader in hospital management and marketing and is President of Presbyterian-University of Pennsylvania Medical Center in Philadelphia. Prior to assuming this position, he was Administrator of St. Mary Hospital in Philadelphia; and before that, Assistant Director of Thomas Jefferson University Hospital, also in Philadelphia.

Mr. Snook has contributed numerous articles to health care management literature and is the author of the widely-read books, *Hospitals: What They Are and How They Work,* and *Building a Winning Medical Staff.* A new book titled, *50 Effective Hospital Print Ads,* was recently published. He is the originator of the "hotel-hospital" concept. He is the recipient of the American Healthcare Marketing Association's "CEO Marketer of the Year Award."

Mr. Snook holds a BBA in Marketing from the Wharton School of the University of Pennsylvania (cum laude), and an MBA in Hospital Administration from George Washington University. He has also completed the Health Management Systems Program at the Harvard Business School. In addition, he is a faculty member in the graduate program in Health Care Administration at LaSalle College in Philadelphia and a Fellow in the American College of Healthcare Executives. Mr. Snook has conducted seminars on physician recruitment and medical staff development and marketing nationally.

EDITA M. KAYE is President and CEO of Kaye Associates Inc., a health care marketing, publishing and public relations firm headquartered in New York City. Ms. Kaye has more than 15 years experience in the health care field, first as a medical journalist, author of over 300 articles for both health care and business publications, and as president of her own agency and publishing firm.

Ms. Kaye is also Associate Editor of the *Hospital Entrepreneur's Newsletter,* and co-author of *Everything You Wanted To Know About PVD* (Ephram Publishing Company, 1986), *The Joint Ventures Textbook* (Aspen, 1987), *Health Care Sales Force* (College of Health Care Executives, 1986), *101 Ways To Get and Keep New Patients* (Smiles Publishing, 1984), *Gadgets, Gimmicks and Other Dental Specialties* (Smiles Publishing, 1984). In addition, she is a frequent contributor to the key health care and business publications on the topics of the changing health care economy.